# ALLA FRATELLI

# ALLA FRATELLI

## How To Eat Italian

### Barry McDonald
with Terry Durack

MURDOCH BOOKS

PRIMAVERA

POMMERY BRUT AP

Salt & Pepper
Squid $18

ALIAN CHEESES $4.95 each.

I PASTI MISTI 16
ETTATI MISTI 19.50
ELLO TONNATO 18
HEART TOMATO
SCIUTTO DI PARMA
VED BABY CABBAG
NONNI "TALEGGIO & MIXE
CKEN LIVER PATE W
WED ZUCCHINI
OF SALAD W PE
KED TROUT SALA
ING PEA SALAD
SOIA" RICOTTA W
CHED CHICKEN
CHED SALMON

BAGNA AL
ATBALLS IN
UINE W PIPIS ARUC
RECCIA W EGG ANT, T
RAGÙ W CHILLI ROSEMA
UINE W LEMON CHILLI &
RISOTTO W MINT, PECORI
SPY POLENTA W MIXED MU
HETTI ALLA CARBONARA
TU ALLA BOLOGNESE 2
ROOM RAGÙ W PECORI
N W 1 ENTI

ARED TUNA W AGROD
ESAN CRUMBED CHICKEN S
ECCA W PORCINI & HERBS
E BAKED TROUT W GREEN O

RELLA DI BUFALA 18
D PEACHES & ROCKET 22
BALSAMIC & REGGIANO 18
RRS" SALAD CREAM 18
L TOASTED CIABATTA 20
PECORINO + POACHED EGG 20
NUTS & GORGONZOLA 18
NENUTS & YOGHURT 24
US, PANCETTA, PECORINO + PATATE 22
IED ASPARAGUS 22
RRANTS CHILLI & MINT 20
CUCUMBERS & SEEDED MUSTARD 24

BUCATINI 22
OTATOES 26
WS & RICOTTA 21
?
.25
NZOLA 21

23
RECCHIETTE 24

CONTORNI

GARLIC BREAD
BROCCOLINI W LEMON &
ROAST PUMPKIN W GARL
MIXED LEAF W BIANCO D
ROCKET & PARME
ROSEMARY + CHILLI MARINA
TOMATOES
CHIPS
RADICCHIO

DOLCI 15.5

HAZELNUT SEMI FREDDO W FONDUTA AL
MERANGHA W MIXED BERRIES CHANTILLY CREA
VANILLA PANNACOTTA W CAMPARI CITRUS JEL
LEMON TORTA W PASSIONFRUIT & AMARETTE
RHUBARB & VANILLA BRULEE W BISCO
BANOFFEE TORTA
TIRAMISU
FORMAGGIO
SPAZZACAMINO
VANILLA GELATO 6.50
WILD BERRY SORBE

PERSONALE

*For my daughters, Nina and Grace.*
*In memory of Anders Ousback*
*and John Marsden.*

MIND YOUR HEAD

# CONTENTS

# THE STORY OF FRATELLI FRESH

*La storia di Fratelli Fresh*

——

BARRY McDONALD

I'm very proud of my Italian heritage. The only trouble is, I don't have one. So I sort of adopted one and grew into it rather than being born into it. Instead of telling everyone that I was a proud son of New Zealand who had travelled the short hop across the Tasman to Australia, I started telling people that I was the son of Italian immigrants.

At one point, I was the only non-Italian on the Italian Chamber of Commerce and Industry in Australia. When they gave me an award, I had to stand up and make a speech. I began by saying: 'When my family migrated to Sydney all those years ago, I had to drop the "o" from my name "Mick Donaldo" in order to assimilate.'

My name is McDonald, right? But suddenly everyone started cheering and applauding, and I didn't have the heart to tell them I was joking.

The truth is I feel Italian. I love Italian food. I adore Italian wine. I make Italian hand gestures, and drink my espresso standing up. I love Sophia Loren, Monica Bellucci, Alessandro Del Piero, Francis Ford Coppola, Andrea Bocelli and Dean Martin. Like all Italians, I think coffee is oxygen, the tomato is a gift from heaven and wine makes life bearable - and I'd give them all up in a flash for my family, because family is everything.

For me, it's always been about family; which is a very Italian way of going through life. When I first started as a fruit and vegetable wholesaler with my brother Jamie, we set up our own warehouse at the massive wholesale produce market at Sydney's Flemington. From there, we supplied some of the best chefs in the city, from Neil Perry at Rockpool and Tetsuya Wakuda at Tetsuya's to Matt Moran at Aria and Guillaume Brahimi at the Sydney Opera House. Many of them I count as mates to this day, in spite of all the times they've rung me to have a good yell about not getting their heirloom tomatoes or baby fennel bulbs. Some chefs take it as a personal insult when the season changes and they have to rewrite their menus.

The market wasn't as multicultural as it is now; it was very, very Italian, and southern Italian at that. After work, at about 5am or 6am, I'd naturally gravitate to the great Italian delis there that are the heart and soul of the market, hanging out with all the old guys and just talking about family, about the price of tomatoes, about football; all the important stuff. I learnt a lot from them; not sure what they learned from me. To this day, I love standing al banco, at a bar, with a bit of salsiccie on a panino in one hand and a coffee in the other, doing business.

The Italian way of doing things was so important to us that when we shifted our business into a big two-level warehouse in Waterloo in 2004, it seemed only natural to give it an Italian name. So Fratelli Fresh (the Fresh Brothers) was born. The idea was to open a retail Italian market and run it in pretty much the same way we ran the wholesale side on the same premises - no fuss, no mess, no big expensive fit-out;

*'The truth is I feel Italian. I love Italian food. I adore Italian wine. I make Italian hand gestures, and drink my espresso standing up.'*

just 'Here are the best fruit and vegetables we can buy: take it or leave it.'

At one stage, we had Australians, Italians, Indonesians, Vietnamese, Thais, Africans, Chinese, Poles, Latvians and Lithuanians on staff. All our packers were Thai, because, like Italians, they're all about food and family. They just know, when they're packing an order, whether the papaya is going to be ripe for today or for tomorrow. They got into the swing of the whole Italian thing, too, and started calling each other Roberto, Giuseppe, Enrico and Rinaldo. That's very Australian. All our delivery drivers were from New Zealand back then, and I only found out later that not one of them had an Australian driver's licence. They were challenging times.

Six weeks after opening, we launched Café Sopra (literally, the cafe upstairs). Sopra was never going to be a restaurant, it was always going to be a cafe where you could drop in, have a coffee and a freshly made panini, and do a bit of shopping while you were there, just like at the market in the old days. Well that was the idea, but things soon took on their own momentum.

Our founding chef, Andy Bunn, who had worked with me at Fuel in Surry Hills, came on board; my wife Karen did the buying of Italian kitchen and homewares; and my daughter Nina came back from running restaurants in London. My dad, Tom, came in and made jams and sauces from the fruit and veg we had left over.

We had two in the kitchen, two on the floor, and I bought the whole kitchen second-hand at auction a couple of weeks before. The liquor licence hadn't quite come through, so I couldn't sell wine. When people started coming in, we'd just give them a glass of wine, no charge. Pretty good value, when you think about it, but it could have sent me broke.

Café Sopra, it turned out, was the key to the whole business, because it pulled everything and everyone together. The menu was driven by whatever produce was on the shelves, so it changed every day. People came to eat, and then shopped on their way out. They'd come here for lunch and eat salumi and polenta, then at the end of the meal, they'd eyeball the big blackboard menu and go off to the shelves and buy the ingredients for something they'd seen.

The chefs had a marketplace under their noses, so the food was defined by seasonality right from day one. They just ran downstairs to see what was on the shelves before they worked out what the lunch specials would be that day. If it was parsnip season, they'd do roast parsnip, and parsnip soup, and parsnip side dishes. If our suppliers had found the first of the pine mushrooms under the trees, they'd go straight into the pasta, risotto and soup. Even the cocktails were fruit-based, to use what we had and what was in season. We had no printed menus, but there were these huge boards left around from the previous tenant, so I just painted them with blackboard paint and used them as over-sized menus; the way we've always listed specials at the market. You just cross out what's been sold, so things keep moving. We still do everything on chalkboards; it's become our trademark.

When Café Sopra opened, it had 70 seats. It was always full and there was always a queue of people waiting. By the time we left Danks Street in 2013, it seated 170 people, and it was always full, too. Now there are three Fratelli Fresh stores, five Café Sopras, and Café Nice, specialising in the French/Italian cooking of the south of France. We do about 10,000 to 12,000 covers a week, and have an amazing team that is part of the one big family, including our current head chef, Sean Corkery, who helped put together the recipes in this book.

The Italianness of Fratelli keeps growing, and these days, there is a real Italian buzz about the place. It started when we hired one Italian, then another. They talked to their friends and family back in Italy, and soon, more came to join them. They often come from the same region - say, all from Milan one year, and Emilia-Romagna the next. Many of the people we have sponsored now live permanently in Australia, with most still working for us. It's nice, because that means they already have a sense of community here. Not everybody likes it, however.

———

*'The chefs had a marketplace under their noses, so the food was defined by seasonality right from day one.'*

———

A customer once emailed me to complain that the girls at the checkout were talking to each other in Italian. 'We are in Australia,' she said. 'Why can't they speak English?' I couldn't believe anyone would have a problem like that in this day and age, but I wrote a very long answer back to explain our point of view. Mind you, I wrote it in Italian.

A lot of the Italian things we do in Sydney are better than how Italians do them in Italy. I really believe that. As much as I love Tuscany, all you can eat there is Tuscan food. In Rome, the Roman food is best. In Milan, the Milanese food. The acclaimed Italian chef Giorgio Locatelli, who grew up in a remote village on the shores of Lake Maggiore in northern Italy, claims his grandfather never tasted fresh chilli in his life, and thought of it as 'foreign food'. In the same way, there are southern Italians who have never tasted polenta or eaten risotto alla Milanese.

But in Australia, we feel free to pick the best ideas and the best food from all over Italy, and turn it out in the way we want to eat it here. So we do pizza, from the south, and polenta, from the north. There's a certain freedom in running an Italian restaurant a long way from Italy. We respect Italian tradition, but not when it gets in the way of something better. In Italy, they still look at you strangely if you order your spaghetti as a main course. Here, we don't mind at all when people order pasta or risotto as a main course in its own right, instead of as a first course. Or if they order a whole pile of antipasti dishes and make a meal of it. Why not?

The opening scene in the 1996 Italian/American film *Big Night* is built on the idea of the chef/owner of a struggling trattoria being too proud to serve consecutive courses of pasta and risotto to one of his customers. He loses the customer, and keeps his pride in Italian cuisine and tradition intact. But he also (spoiler alert) loses the restaurant.

We do things differently here from the old country - and from the new country, come to think of it.

That's why we called our book *Alla Fratelli* - in the way of Fratelli. Our food is so simple, it means the quality of the ingredients is the most important thing. You can't mess with that. Fresh is best. In season is best. Italian is best.

# SHOP LIKE AN ITALIAN
*Comprare come un Italiano*

Nobody goes to the market in Italy with a shopping list, unless they're shopping for a wedding. They don't need a list, because they have their eyes. They can see for themselves what's best, and they can tell what's in season because there's lots of it. Cavolo nero and mushrooms and truffles in winter. Strawberries and peaches in summer. They use their noses, too. Even the fish section in a good market smells good, with a fabulous fresh, ocean smell. I remember walking along a market aisle in Florence one day and being hit with this intensely sweet smell, as if I'd walked into a flower farm. It took me three more metres to find out it was coming from a tiny stall of wild strawberries. Now, when the Kensington Pride mangoes from Bowen in Queensland are on, I always put a pallet of them right in the doorway of Fratelli Fresh. The smell drives people crazy.

Italians like to shop for the day, and not for the week. So they go to the same shops and the same market stalls every morning; they say hello, have a coffee. It's a social outing as well as a shopping trip. It keeps them alive, keeps them young.

Like market shoppers everywhere, they haggle, but they don't haggle about price - they haggle about quality. They point to the exact piece of fruit or vegetable that they want, and simply won't settle for anything else. What they don't do in Italy is touch and prod and squeeze the fruit and vegetables. As the sign says, 'Si prega di non toccare la merce esposta.' Please don't touch the merchandise.

And once they know what they're going to buy, they know what they're going to cook.

There's a symbiotic relationship between Italians and markets. I head straight for the markets when I'm travelling in Italy, before I go to any art galleries or museums. They're my churches; I feel at home there, as if I know the people already. And even though I'm staying in hotels, I can't help but buy bunches of tiny, scented basil, a donkey salami, a bag of wild mushrooms, just because I can.

The Mercato Centrale in Florence, the amazing Neo-Gothic Rialto Market in Venice, the beautiful Campo dei Fiore in Rome... they're not tourist attractions, but wheeling, dealing parts of Italian daily life.

In Australia you get to the wholesale market at 4am or everything will be gone. But Italy doesn't get up that early. At the Campo dei Fiore, for instance, things don't kick off until about 7am. So I always get there too early, but it gives me a chance to catch the setting-up, which is fascinating. All these little cobblestone streets that converge onto the piazza and the stallholders coming in from every direction with their carts and their three-wheeled scooter trucks loaded high with wooden boxes and plastic crates. It's mayhem, as they're setting up and raising the canopies and waiters from the nearby cafes come rushing in with trays of coffee, yet it works.

———

*'Nobody goes to the market in Italy with a shopping list, unless they're shopping for a wedding. They don't need a list, because they have their eyes.'*

———

Families run a lot of the stalls. First you see the kids, then you see the parents, and then finally the grandmother turns up. You can tell these people have been doing this forever. They are absolutely meticulous in their preparation. I watch as they peel back their lettuces, check over their fruit and trim the artichokes ready for sale. Every piece of fruit is placed individually. It really is an art.

I remember one woman who was selling parsley at so much per 100 grams. She was breaking off bunches, putting it on the scales, taking one sprig off, putting two on, until it was spot on. All this effort for something like 20 cents.

By 1.30pm, the market is winding down and the council trucks move in. The cleaning-up operation is like a finely honed military exercise, in contrast to the mayhem of setting up. The nearby cafes start putting out their chairs, and the local kids often drift into the square to play football.

At night, the place is a party, and the piazza turns into a kind of natural amphitheatre as the street musicians and performers come to entertain all the al fresco diners. Then there is an hour or two of silence, before the carts and the trucks and the whole thing starts all over again. There's a rhythm to it all.

I don't go to the wholesale markets every day any more, but what you learn never leaves you. I can't walk past a display without checking it, improving it. I have to stop myself rearranging the apples in the supermarket.

When you're in the business, you can tell when things aren't as fresh as they seem, because you know all the tricks. You can tell when the tired bits have been cut away or when the asparagus has been trimmed back. The real give-away is the radicchio. In a lot of markets, you can come back every day and watch the radicchio get smaller and smaller and smaller as they trim off the dead leaves. So clever shoppers go where the turnover is greatest, not smallest.

If I had to give people advice on shopping, it would be to use your eyes, ears and nose, not just your hands. Over time, you get a feel for great produce; it stands out, it ticks all the boxes and you know you just have to have it.

*'Over time, you get a feel for great produce; it stands out, it ticks all the boxes and you know you just have to have it.'*

GREEN
CAPSICUM $7.95 Kg

LADY FINGER

# EAT LIKE AN ITALIAN
## Mangiare come un Italiano

I love how when you turn up to lunch at an Italian friend's place, there's no food to be seen.

Just as you start to get worried, a dish of olives comes out and you have a bit of a nibble on them. Then someone gets up and disappears and comes back with a platter of finely sliced prosciutto or bresaola, and maybe some crisp, thin grissini.

More time goes by, and more talk, then out comes a bowl of roasted red peppers or eggplant under vinegar. Maybe some bread, maybe not. Some ripe figs, or crisp pears, depending on the season. A hunk of cheese.

By this time, you're quite happy to have a coffee and go home. That, of course, is when they bring out the big, steaming bowls of pasta. And that's just the primi, the first course.

After that, often quite some time after that, comes the secondo, or main course, which is usually really, really simple: just some meat in its own cooking juices, or a whole grilled fish and a salad. The secondo is usually accompanied by contorni, or side dishes. Maybe there'll be a bowl of tender white beans on the side, tossed with rosemary and gleaming with rich extra virgin olive oil.

After that, there might be a bowl of fruit, or a little slice of cake with an oily black espresso coffee. Then just when you think you should be getting going, a little silver tray of glasses will appear with a lethal homemade liqueur that will blow your head off. And some crunchy little biscotti.

Italians don't really believe in breakfast (you can see why). It's usually a cup of coffee taken with a little pastry, a cornetto (croissant) or a cigarette. They still smoke in Italy.

Lunch is traditionally the main meal of the day, and dinner is often lighter and simpler. The old custom of the man leaving work in the middle of the day and calling his stay-at-home wife to put the water on for the pasta is dying out now. But there is still the ritual of the Sunday family lunch at home. Apparently, only five per cent of Italians eat out on a Sunday; instead, they all go to their mother's. And of course, there's la passeggiata, the slow stroll after the meal, in equal parts to aid the digestion and to check out what everyone's wearing on the street.

In Italy, it's as much about how you eat as what you eat. Italians are quite formal at the table; they take care of their elders, and make the kids welcome. If you sit and watch an Italian family at the table, you'll see there's a lot of touching, hugging and kissing, a lot of eye contact, a lot of respect for each other. They give themselves time to get together, time to eat, and time to digest their food.

I reckon a lot of the real benefits of the Mediterranean diet are as much due to taking this time, as they are to the use of olive oil and the popularity of grains and greens. I also think that Italians really benefit - they have one of the longest life spans in the world - by simply being passionate about their food and wine. Ars vivendi - it's the art of living your life with passion. When you prioritise something like food and wine so strongly, you don't let your standards slip into eating junk food or drinking too much.

We're so lucky in Australia to be surrounded by so much good food and so many options that we take it for granted. But you can tell, behind every Italian's big personality and big, generous table, there's a tiny, tiny fear that the good life will be taken away from them, that life could one day be hard, and that nothing should be taken for granted. It's this sense of history that makes them appreciate good food and wine. So much of their connection to food is through festivals and religious days and family; it's very celebratory, as if every day will be their last.

It won't be, of course, but it means they make the most of everything that comes their way.

# DRINK LIKE AN ITALIAN
## *Bere come un Italiano*

In all my trips to Italy and hanging around in bars - doing important research - I don't think I've ever seen an Italian who has had too much to drink.

Italians seem to treat alcohol as a special occasion, even if that special occasion happens every single day. Nobody drinks to get drunk. Glasses are small, not large. Drinking is always seen as an integral part of eating and being with other people, rather than as a substitute for either. There's no showing off, just a clear understanding that wine is a part of life.

The best way to drink like an Italian is to know your befores and afters. Before the meal, the aperitivo reigns supreme, and after the meal, the digestivo takes over. There are serious reasons for both: one to stimulate the gastric juices before the stomach has to digest the food; and the latter to help with the digestive process.

I haven't seen any research on the scientific proof of either theory, but I'm not convinced that's important. It just makes sense.

The thing about aperitivo, derived from the Latin aperitivus, to open, is that it refers to both the drink itself and the occasion surrounding the drinking. Milan started the habit, apparently, by lining the bar with platters of snacks and bowls of crisps to entice people in for a drink at the end of the working day. Different cities call this different things, from spuntini to stuzzichini to the Venetian cicchetti. Look out for it in Milan, Turin and Florence, where chic little bars will lay on a spread of cheeses, salumi, pastries and nibbly bits between 7pm and 9pm.

The custom has grown, more recently, into a bit of a free-for-all buffet for the price of an (expensive) cocktail, which is a bit of a shame, and not half as classy. I prefer it when it is more elegant, and spare; just a few well-chosen things, put together with care, and eaten over time, and over talk. To drink like an Italian, to me, is to pay attention to detail.

The lovely, heart-warming thing about Italians is how they surround the smallest act - pouring a drink - with a sense of occasion, and with its own little set of rituals and unspoken rules. The aperitivo itself can be just a glass of prosecco. However, it's more likely to involve one of the bitter liquors that Italians find themselves drawn to, such as Campari, Aperol or vermouth; either straight, over ice, or in classic cocktails such as the negroni, the Americano and the cin cin.

The spritz is a light aperitivo popular in northern Italy and especially in Venice, made with prosecco, a dash of either Campari or Aperol and a top-up of sparkling mineral water. And there's beer, of course. Any of the famous Italian brands of Moretti, Peroni and Menabrea are just the thing before a crusty pizza.

Cutting straight to after the meal, it's time for a digestivo, also known as an ammazzacaffe ('coffee killer') if taken after an after-dinner espresso. These also lean towards the bitter; the almost medicinal liqueurs made from jealously guarded recipes involving bitter herbs, roots, plants and spices. There could be an Averna or some other brand of amaro with its distinctive herbal bitterness. Then there's the artichoke-based Cynar, the outrageously bitter and vaguely minty Fernet-Branca and Ramazzotti, which includes no fewer than 30 herbs and roots in its maceration. Limoncello is often homemade from sun-dried lemons and offered at the end of a meal; it's good when it's not too sweet. A shot of grappa, a high-proof wine liquor made from pressed grapes, is like a breath of pure oxygen at the end of a traditional five-course Italian meal. It's also a cheeky little addition to many an espresso in the early morning, when it is known as a caffe corretto - the coffee having been 'corrected' by the slug of grappa. I suspect grappa is the sole secret to Italy's survival. If you can drink that, you can do anything.

# APERITIVI

My daughter Nina has been looking after the bar and wine side of Café Sopra and Café Nice since she hit legal drinking age - and possibly before that. Like me, she loves how Italians have a way of turning a simple pre-dinner drink into the highlight of the day, by paying attention to detail and presentation - the right glass, the twist of orange, the coaster, the tray. Here are a few of her favourites. Each recipe makes one, so double the quantities if you get lucky.

## ITALIAN SOUR
*Cocktails can - and should - be as seasonal as food.*

30 ml (1 fl oz) Campari
30 ml (1 fl oz) Aperol
15 ml (1/2 fl oz) lemon Chartreuse
15 ml (1/2 fl oz) sugar syrup (Basics, 258)
15 ml (1/2 fl oz) lime or lemon juice
30 ml (1 fl oz) grapefruit juice
grapefruit peel, to serve

Shake all the ingredients on ice, and pour into an old-fashioned glass. Garnish with a twist of grapefruit peel and serve.

## COCO
*Very girly and summery, the Coco is an Italian spin on the Cosmopolitan - but without the cranberry.*

30 ml (1 fl oz) vodka
30 ml (1 fl oz) Cointreau
30 ml (1 fl oz) watermelon juice
dash of lime cordial
dash of sugar syrup (Basics, 258)
Pommery Brut Royal NV Champagne, to serve
watermelon pieces, to serve

Shake all the ingredients except the Champagne on ice. Pour into a tall glass and top with Pommery Brut or an equivalent premium Champagne. Garnish with a small piece of watermelon and serve.

## NEGRONI
*We make our Negroni with Carpano Antica Formula, which is richer and more complex than most Italian vermouths.*

20 ml (1/2 fl oz) Campari
20 ml (1/2 fl oz) gin
20 ml (1/2 fl oz) Carpano Antica Formula
orange peel, to serve

Pour all the ingredients over ice in an old-fashioned glass. Stir, then garnish with a twist of orange peel and serve.

## AMERICANO
*This was invented by Gaspare Campari - we owe him so much. The first Americano was served at Milan's Caffè Campari in the 1860s, when it was known as the 'Milano-Torino'.*

30 ml (1 fl oz) Campari
30 ml (1 fl oz) vermouth rosso
soda water
orange peel, to serve

Stir the Campari and vermouth over ice in an old-fashioned glass. Top with a dash of soda, garnish with a twist of orange peel and serve.

## VESPA
*The Vespa manages to be both bitter and sweet at the same time, a little in the style of an Italian cola - except this has the advantage of being alcoholic.*

30 ml (1 fl oz) dry vermouth
15 ml (1/2 fl oz) amaretto
Angostura bitters
limonata, to serve
sliced lemon, to serve

Pour all the ingredients over ice in an old-fashioned glass. Stir, then top with a dash of limonata. Garnish with a lemon slice and serve.

## SPRITZ

*This is not just the flavour of the month, it's the flavour of every month. It's the biggest-selling cocktail throughout the Café Sopra family, and a big hit at our staff Christmas parties. The Campari Spritz is a touch more bitter than the Aperol.*

40 ml (1¼ fl oz) Aperol or Campari
60 ml (2 fl oz) prosecco
soda water, to serve
sliced orange, to serve

Pour the Aperol and prosecco over ice in a wine glass. Top with a dash of soda, garnish with an orange slice and serve.

## ESPRESSO MARTINI

*Delicious to drink and easy to make, the kick of caffeine and the lushness of the Kahlua in this makes it an equally good choice before or after dinner. Or even during, if that's your thing.*

30 ml (1 fl oz) vodka
30 ml (1 fl oz) Kahlua
2 shots espresso coffee, cooled
coffee beans, to serve

Shake the vodka, Kahlua and coffee on ice, and strain into a chilled martini glass. Garnish with three coffee beans and serve.

## BELLINI

*Invented in 1948, at Harry's Bar in Venice, by Giuseppe Cipriani, this is a seasonal treasure.*

60 ml (2 fl oz) prosecco
30 ml (1 fl oz) peach puree

Add a dash of the prosecco to the peach puree, and stir until mixed. Pour into a Champagne glass, and carefully top with the remaining prosecco.

## ITALIAN ICED TEA

*Once you see one of these go out to someone else at the bar, it's almost impossible not to order one for yourself. For me, it conjures up visions of southern Italians sitting on a beach - always a compelling image.*

15 ml (½ fl oz) gin
15 ml (½ fl oz) vodka
15 ml (½ fl oz) amaretto
15 ml (½ fl oz) white rum
squeeze of lemon juice
chinotto, to serve
sliced orange, to serve

Fill a tall glass with ice cubes, then add the ingredients one by one. Finish with a dash of chinotto, garnish with a slice of orange and serve.

## STRAWBERRY BALSAMIC SMASH

*When Nina started raiding the produce shelves in search of the perfect summer cocktail, she hit on strawberries and balsamic vinegar, and loved it. I won't share with you some of the other experimental fruit and vegetable cocktails she came up with (the zucchini was perhaps a step too far) but don't let me stop you from getting more fruit and veg in your diet.*

2 fresh strawberries
2 basil leaves, plus extra to serve
2 lime wedges
45 ml (1½ fl oz) Absolut vodka
15 ml (½ fl oz) Fragole strawberry liqueur
dash of balsamic vinegar
15 ml (½ fl oz) sugar syrup (Basics, 258)

Muddle the strawberries, basil and lime in a cocktail mixing glass. Add the vodka, Fragole, balsamic vinegar and sugar syrup, and shake with ice. Pour into a glass (or glass jar), garnish with a basil leaf and serve.

ARANCINI w TALEGGIO
CAPONATA w PINENUTS

# ANTIPASTI

WARM ROSEMARY OLIVES
PEA & PECORINO CROSTINI
ZUCCHINI FLOWERS w 5 HALIAN
CHEESES

# ARANCINI WITH TALEGGIO

**SERVES 4 AS ANTIPASTI**

*They're crunchy, they're hot and they're gone in a bite or two. And these more-ish little rice balls give you a false sense of security that you haven't really had that much to drink, because they soak up the vino like crazy.*

500 ml (17 fl oz/2 cups) chicken or vegetable
   stock (Basics, 259)
40 g (1½ oz) butter, chopped
1½ tbsp extra virgin olive oil
1½ onions, finely chopped
4 garlic cloves, finely chopped
250 g (9 oz) arborio or carnaroli rice
200 ml (7 fl oz) white wine
handful flat-leaf parsley leaves, chopped
1 bunch chives, chopped
1 bunch mint leaves, chopped
55 g (2 oz) parmesan, finely grated, plus extra to serve
100 g (3½ oz) taleggio
100 g (3½ oz) plain (all-purpose) flour
2 eggs, lightly whisked
125 g (4½ oz) dry breadcrumbs
vegetable oil, for deep-frying
lemon, cut into wedges

*'Antipasti is a rolling feast that changes day to day, week by week, like an Italian market stall.'*

To make the risotto, bring the stock to the boil in a large saucepan, then maintain it at a gentle simmer.

Heat the butter and olive oil in a heavy-based saucepan over low-medium heat.

Add the onion and garlic and cook for 8 minutes or until translucent, stirring occasionally. Add the rice and stir for a further 2 minutes until well coated in the mixture.

Add the wine and simmer until evaporated, then add the hot stock, a ladleful at a time, to the rice, stirring continuously and allowing the stock to be absorbed before adding the next. Do this until all the stock has been used, the rice is cooked and the mixture is thick, about 20 minutes. Stir in all the herbs and parmesan until combined. Cool slightly, then spread on a tray and refrigerate for 2 hours or until chilled.

To shape the arancini, roll tablespoons of the risotto into balls. Pull off 1 cm (½ in) pieces of taleggio and press into the centre of each ball, then re-roll to enclose the taleggio.

Place the flour, egg and breadcrumbs in different bowls.

Lightly dust the arancini in the flour, dip into the egg and roll in the breadcrumbs until evenly coated.

Fill a wok or deep saucepan one-third full with oil and heat to 180°C (350°F).

Deep-fry the arancini in batches, for 3 minutes, turning constantly, or until golden and heated through. Drain on paper towel and serve with lemon wedges and a little extra grated parmesan.

# CAPONATA WITH PINE NUTS

**SERVES 4 AS ANTIPASTI**

*One for lovers of eggplant, this rustic, stewy mess of vegetables is beautiful served at room temperature or with a simple grill of fish or meat.*

2 tbsp extra virgin olive oil
2 shallots, roughly chopped
2 garlic cloves, finely sliced
1 celery stalk, roughly chopped
1/4 red capsicum (pepper), roughly chopped
1/2 eggplant (aubergine), chopped
200 g (7 oz) tinned chopped tomatoes
2 tsp red wine vinegar
1 tsp caster (superfine) sugar
1 tbsp pine nuts, toasted
1 tbsp sultanas
4 green olives, pitted, roughly chopped
1 tsp salted baby capers, rinsed
4 basil leaves, chopped

Heat the olive oil in a frying pan and cook the shallots, garlic and celery for 5 minutes. Add the capsicum and eggplant and cook for a further 5 minutes. Add the tomatoes and simmer for 15 minutes or until thickened. Add the vinegar and sugar and cook for 2 more minutes, stirring. Check for seasoning, and stir in the pine nuts, sultanas, olives, capers and basil. Serve warm.

# COZZE RIPIENE

**SERVES 6 AS ANTIPASTI**

*A plate of these golden, garlicky, crumb-topped mussels, and a glass of Italian chardonnay or Soave, and really, you don't need much after that.*

350 g (12 oz) loaf day-old, rustic-style bread
2 garlic cloves, finely grated
2 tbsp chopped flat-leaf parsley leaves
1 tsp dried oregano
finely grated zest of 1 lemon
4 tbsp extra virgin olive oil
2 kg (4 lb 8 oz) fresh black mussels, scrubbed, bearded

First make the crumb mixture. Remove the crust from the bread then roughly chop the bread. Process in a food processor until coarse crumbs form.

Tip the crumbs into a bowl and combine with the garlic, parsley, oregano and lemon zest, then season with sea salt and freshly ground black pepper. Drizzle with 3 tablespoons of the olive oil and toss to combine.

Heat the grill (broiler) to medium-high.

Discard any broken mussels, or opened ones that don't close when tapped on the bench.

Place the mussels in a large, wide saucepan, cover tightly and cook over high heat for 2-3 minutes, shaking the pan occasionally. Uncover the pan and remove the mussels with a slotted spoon as they open.

Remove the meat from half the mussels and discard the shells. Open the remaining mussels wide, keeping both half-shells attached, then place on a baking tray.

Place one of the removed mussels - two if small - on the empty half of each shell.

Top the mussels with 1 tablespoon of the crumbs and grill until golden.

Drizzle with the remaining olive oil and serve hot.

# WARM ROSEMARY OLIVES

**SERVES 10 AS ANTIPASTI**

*This couldn't be simpler, but like a good guest at a party, warm, rosemary-scented olives make everything around them more interesting.*

500 ml (17 fl oz/2 cups) extra virgin olive oil
350 g (12 oz) kalamata olives
350 g (12 oz) Sicilian (small, black) olives
2 garlic cloves, sliced
1 fresh long mild red chilli, split down the middle
1/4 bunch thyme, leaves picked
1/4 bunch rosemary, leaves picked
2 bay leaves
1 tsp whole black peppercorns

In a large saucepan, heat the olive oil gently to 50°C (120°F) and remove from the heat. Add the remaining ingredients, then allow to cool to room temperature.

Spoon into airtight jars, cover with the oil and store in the fridge for up to 2 weeks.

Gently re-warm in a little of the oil to serve.

# EGGPLANT CAVIAR

**SERVES 4 AS ANTIPASTI**

*We serve this with bresaola - salt-cured, air-dried beef; in this case, the rich, marbled wagyu that's the amazing Australian version of the Japanese kobe beef - and plenty of freshly grated Parmigiano Reggiano. It's an instant umami hit.*

2 eggplant (aubergine), cut in half lengthways
2 tbsp vegetable oil
2 garlic cloves, finely sliced
3 shallots, sliced
2 tomatoes
1/2 bunch coriander (cilantro), leaves and stalks finely chopped
100 ml (3½ fl oz) lemon vinaigrette (Basics, 254)
extra virgin olive oil, to serve

Heat the oven to 180°C (350°F). Wrap the eggplant in foil and bake for 45 minutes or until soft and tender. Unwrap and cool. Spoon out the flesh into a colander and allow to drain for 1 hour.

In a small frying pan, heat the vegetable oil and cook the garlic and shallot with a pinch of sea salt until soft. Transfer to a mixing bowl.

Cut the tomatoes in half and squeeze out and discard the seeds. Cut into 1 cm (½ in) dice and toss with the garlic and shallot.

Add the drained eggplant and the coriander, tossing well. Add the lemon vinaigrette, season with sea salt and freshly ground black pepper and serve.

# PEA & PECORINO CROSTINI

**SERVES 4 AS ANTIPASTI**

*Crostini could be translated as 'good things on toast'; the perfect bite with that first glass of wine. We love this fresh, pea-green version with grated pecorino.*

4 slices ficelle or baguette
2 tbsp extra virgin olive oil
100 g (3½ oz) fresh peas, podded
4 mint leaves, chopped
grated pecorino, to serve

Heat the oven to 160°C (315°F). Place the sliced bread on a baking tray, drizzle with half the olive oil and bake for 6-8 minutes or until crisp and golden.

Cook the peas in boiling, salted water for 3 minutes or until just tender. Drain and refresh in iced water to stop the cooking.

Roughly crush the peas with the remaining olive oil, sea salt and freshly ground black pepper, fold in the mint and spoon onto the crostini. Top with pecorino and serve.

# TORTA DI MELANZANE

**SERVES 6**

*I think dishes like this baked eggplant pie define your restaurant. It's simple, with very few ingredients, and yet it's generous, dishing up really big flavours.*

500 ml (17 fl oz/2 cups) tomato passata
100 g (3½ oz) parmesan, finely grated
60 g (2¼ oz) dry breadcrumbs
olive oil, for shallow-frying
4 eggplant (aubergine), cut lengthwise
   into 1 cm (½ in) slices
4 balls buffalo mozzarella, drained, finely sliced

Simmer the tomato passata in a small saucepan over medium heat until reduced by one-third. Allow to cool. Combine the parmesan and breadcrumbs in a bowl.

Heat the olive oil in a large frying pan and shallow-fry the eggplant in batches, adding more oil as necessary, for 2 minutes each side or until golden, then drain on paper towel. Season with sea salt and black pepper.

Heat the oven to 190°C (375°F).

To assemble the pie, fan out the eggplant slices so they overlap across the base of a heavy-based, ovenproof 22 cm (8½ in) diameter frying pan and reach 2 cm (¾ in) up the sides. Spoon over one-third of the reduced passata, then scatter with one-third of the parmesan mixture. Place half the mozzarella on top.

Repeat the layering, finishing with the mozzarella, then spoon over the remaining passata and eggplant to cover the top.

Scatter with the remaining parmesan mixture and bake for 35 minutes or until heated through. Set aside for several hours or until at room temperature.

To serve, either turn out onto a plate and cut into slices, or cut into slices straightaway from the pan and serve with a green salad.

# ZUCCHINI FLOWERS WITH FIVE ITALIAN CHEESES

**SERVES 4–6**

*You can't go wrong with this. It looks pretty. It uses five cheeses inside, and parmesan outside. People love it; it's our biggest seller. Why male zucchini flowers? Because the males don't have a zucchini attached to them like the females, so you're not trashing a future zucchini.*

200 g (7 oz) fresh ricotta
60 g (2¼ oz) pecorino, grated
40 g (1½ oz) taleggio, chopped
20 g (¾ oz) gorgonzola dolce, chopped
20 g (¾ oz) parmesan, grated, plus extra to serve
12 male zucchini (courgette) flowers
vegetable oil, for deep-frying

**BATTER**
250 g (9 oz) plain (all-purpose) flour
455 ml (16 fl oz) sparkling mineral water

To make the batter, place the flour in a bowl and gradually whisk in the mineral water to make a light, smooth batter. Set aside.

Meanwhile, place the ricotta, pecorino, taleggio, gorgonzola and parmesan in a bowl and use a wooden spoon to mix to a paste.

Gently open each zucchini flower and trim the stem to 2 cm (¾ in). Fill each flower with 1 tablespoon of the cheese mixture, then pull the petals over the filling to enclose.

With the palm of your hand, flatten each one slightly to splay the petals; the filling will become slightly exposed.

Fill a deep-fryer or saucepan one-third full with vegetable oil and heat over medium heat to 180°C (350°F).

Working in three batches, dip the flowers into the batter, allowing the batter to drain off, then gently drop the flowers into the oil and fry for 3 minutes, turning halfway through cooking, or until pale golden. Drain well on paper towel, and keep warm in the oven while cooking the rest. Serve with extra grated parmesan.

# SALUMI

Salumi is a share thing. It's a great way to start a meal. The meats also need to be freshly sliced, so find a really good butcher or deli - or come and order it at Café Sopra instead. These are our all-time favourites:

*Prosciutto crudo* is cured ham, as opposed to prosciutto cotto, which is cooked ham. Prosciutto is made from the hind leg of the pig, salted then hung for 12-16 months. The best known are prosciutto di Parma from Emilia-Romagna and the nutty, silky prosciutto San Daniele from Friuli. Prosciutto should be sliced as thinly as possible to get a good balance of meat and fat. Prosciutto e melone is the classic antipasto, but it is also excellent simply draped over tomato bruschetta.

*Salame* is the generic term for a range of salt-cured sausages, or insaccati (literally 'bagged goods'), mostly made from pork and cured. Every region makes its own particular salame, ranging from the relatively delicate salame di Milano in the north to the robust, fiery salsiccia Calabrese of the south.

*Bresaola* is a specialty of Valtellina in Lombardy: a salt-cured, air-dried beef that should be sliced very thinly and served with a little lemon juice and freshly ground black pepper.

*Nduja* (pronounced en-doo-ya) is a soft, spreadable and very hot salami from Calabria in Italy's south. It can be served as part of an antipasti or salumi platter, spread on pizza, baked into bread, or added to pasta, soups and slow braises.

*Mortadella* is the largest of the Italian salume, weighing up to 15 kilograms. Basically, it's an extremely elegant combination of 70 per cent pork and 30 per cent pork fat and a few spices. It can be finely sliced and eaten as part of an affettati (sliced meat) platter, or used in pasta stuffings and meatball mixtures.

*Coppa* is cured and air-dried pork neck or pig's shoulder, and needs to age for about 3 months. It tastes a little like prosciutto but earthier and leaner.

## AFFETTATI MISTI
### SERVES 4

*Affettati misti means 'sliced and mixed' and generally refers to cured meats. It sounds so ordinary, yet it's one of the best things in the world, especially when it's served with crusty bread and crisp grissini.*

100 g (3½ oz) mortadella, finely sliced
50 g (1¾ oz) wagyu bresaola, finely sliced
50 g (1¾ oz) prosciutto, finely sliced
50 g (1¾ oz) salami, finely sliced
1 tbsp extra virgin olive oil
1 lemon, cut into wedges

Arrange the meats on a large platter in a way that will best showcase all the different colours and textures. Drizzle with the olive oil and scatter with freshly ground black pepper. Serve with lemon wedges.

*'The most important thing about cured meat is the fineness of the slice - it needs to be precise and delicate.'*

OXHEART TOMATO

MOZZARELLA DI BUFALA

OSTINI w 'NDUJA, BOCCONCINI

# MOZZARELLA

BURRATA w BROAD BEANS &
CELERY HEART

BRUSCHETTA w RICOTTA &
FIELD MUSHROOMS

TRUFFLE SALAMI w AGRODOLCE
ONIONS & MOZZARELLA

Fratelli Fresh
dal 1974
Fratelli Fresh
dal 1974
HIGHLAND
Fetta
Premium
COLD SMOKED SALMON
PICKLED BEETROOT

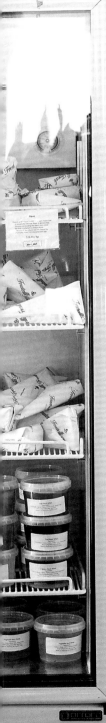

Fratelli Fresh
dal 1974

Fratelli Fresh
dal 1974

Fratelli Fresh
dal 1974

# OX-HEART TOMATOES WITH MOZZARELLA DI BUFALA & BASIL

**SERVES 4**

*To make mozzarella, the curd is broken up and heated in water until it becomes elastic and forms a thread, which is then wound round and round into a ball, from which the pieces are torn off or cut off (the verb mozzare means 'to cut off'). It's at its very best in the classic insalata caprese.*

juice of 1/2 lemon
100 ml (3 1/2 fl oz) extra virgin olive oil
4 ox-heart tomatoes, firm but ripe
2 x 250 g (9 oz) balls buffalo mozzarella, drained
12 basil leaves

In a bowl, whisk together the lemon juice and olive oil with sea salt and freshly ground black pepper. Slice the tomatoes across into four pieces about 5 mm (¼ in) thick. Tear each mozzarella into eight pieces. Season and dress the mozzarella and tomatoes with the lemon oil, and serve piled on a plate, topped with the torn basil.

*'Red. White. Green. It's all about the quality of the tomatoes, the freshness of the mozzarella, and the fragrance of the basil.'*

# BURRATA WITH BROAD BEANS & CELERY HEART

**SERVES 4**

*Burrata is a creamier version of mozzarella from the southern Italian region of Puglia. The cheese-makers form the warm curds into a pouch, then fill the pouch with fresh cream and tie it up like a money bag. It's particularly good served with a simple platter of mixed cured meats, or affettati misti (recipe, 41).*

200 g (7 oz) fresh broad (fava) beans, shelled
1 bunch English spinach
1 head of radicchio
1/2 bunch mint, leaves picked
1 bunch celery
3 tbsp extra virgin olive oil
2 tbsp lemon juice
100 g (3 1/2 oz) burrata, drained

Cook the broad beans in simmering, salted water for 2 minutes or until tender, then drain and cool in iced water to stop the cooking. When cool, peel off the skins and split each bean in two.

Wash the spinach, radicchio and mint, shake dry, and tear by hand into a large bowl. Pick the smaller leaves from the celery, and add to the bowl. Remove the outer stalks (save them for something else) and finely slice the inner, yellow centre part of the plant. Add to the bowl with the broad beans.

Whisk the olive oil, lemon juice, sea salt and freshly ground black pepper, lightly toss through the salad and arrange over plates.

Tear the burrata into rough pieces over the salad and serve, or leave the burrata whole and serve with the leaves.

*'I always say, if you have mozzarella, you have a meal.'*

# BRUSCHETTA WITH RICOTTA & FIELD MUSHROOMS

**SERVES 4**

*Ricotta can be made with the milk of sheep, cows, goats and even buffalo. We love the extra smoothness and creaminess of ricotta di bufala, but any super-fresh, soft, light ricotta would be good here.*

4 large flat mushrooms, trimmed
3 tbsp extra virgin olive oil
4 slices sourdough bread, cut 1 cm (1/2 in) thick
1 garlic clove
250 g (9 oz) ricotta di bufala, drained if necessary
1 handful watercress (optional), sprigs picked

Heat a barbecue or ridged cast-iron grill pan over high heat. Rub the mushrooms with half the olive oil and grill for 3 minutes each side or until tender, then thickly slice.

Brush the bread slices with the remaining olive oil and grill for 2 minutes each side or until charred but not burnt.

Rub the toast slices with the garlic clove, spread generously with the ricotta, and top with the mushroom slices.

Season with sea salt and freshly ground black pepper, top with the watercress (if using), drizzle with a little extra olive oil and serve.

# CROSTINI WITH NDUJA, BOCCONCINI & ROCKET

**SERVES 4**

*Nduja (we Italians say it en-doo-ya) is a soft, spreadable, spicy-hot salami from Calabria in southern Italy. It's great with antipasti, on pizza, with pasta, or spread on hot little oven-baked crostini to have with a drink. It helps if you have a high chilli threshold.*

4 bocconcini or 8 cherry bocconcini (baby mozzarella), drained, chopped
4 thin slices sourdough
2 tbsp olive oil
100 g (3 1/2 oz) nduja, skinned
good handful of rocket (arugula) leaves
extra virgin olive oil, to serve

Heat the oven to 180°C (350°F). Allow the bocconcini to come to room temperature. Brush the bread with the olive oil, season well and bake on a baking tray for 6-8 minutes or until crisped. Remove from the oven and while still hot, spread with the nduja. Top with the bocconcini and rocket, season and drizzle with extra virgin olive oil. Serve immediately.

# TRUFFLE SALAMI WITH AGRODOLCE ONIONS & MOZZARELLA

**SERVES 4**

*Agrodolce simply means 'sweet and sour', something achieved by the right balance of sugar and vinegar. In turn, the sweet-and-sour onions balance the richness of the salami and creaminess of the mozzarella.*

16 button (baby) onions, peeled
2 tbsp olive oil
1 tbsp brown or raw (demerara) sugar
3 tbsp red wine vinegar
1 tbsp currants or sultanas
100 g (3½ oz) truffle salami, thinly sliced
250 g (9 oz) buffalo mozzarella, drained
2½ tbsp extra virgin olive oil

Cook the onions in simmering, salted water for 5-6 minutes or until just tender but not soft. Drain and dry on paper towel.

Heat the olive oil in a saucepan over medium heat, add the onions and cook for 5 minutes or until golden all over. Add the sugar and cook for a further minute or until the sugar has dissolved and starts to caramelise. Carefully add the vinegar and simmer for a further minute. Add the currants and allow to cool in the pan.

To serve, arrange the salami on plates. Spoon the room-temperature onions and their syrup over the top, and scatter with torn chunks of mozzarella.

Drizzle with the extra virgin olive oil, scatter with freshly ground black pepper and serve.

*'Pulling the mozzarella apart with your fingers is always better than using a knife.'*

ROAST TOMATO

CHICKPEA

PASTA & FAGIOLI

ZUPPA

PARSNIP SOUP w GORGONZOLA

PAPPA AL POMODORO

FENNEL SOUP w BASIL

# ROAST TOMATO, FENNEL & CHICKPEA SOUP

**SERVES 4**

*Hot, red and just a little spicy. The great thing about this soup is the extra dimension of flavour you get from roasting the fennel, tomatoes and chilli first; it makes all the difference.*

2 fennel bulbs, trimmed

100 ml (3½ fl oz) olive oil, plus extra to serve

8 roma (plum) tomatoes, halved

1 fresh long red chilli

1 onion, finely chopped

3 garlic cloves, finely sliced

1 bunch basil, leaves picked

1.5 litres (52 fl oz/6 cups) vegetable (Basics, 259) or chicken stock

200 g (7 oz) cooked or tinned chickpeas, rinsed, drained

crusty bread, to serve

Heat the oven to 220°C (425°F). Cut each fennel bulb into quarters. Leaving the core in, cut each quarter into three wedges. Place on a baking tray, drizzle with 2 tablespoons of the olive oil and season. Bake for 15 minutes or until soft and golden.

Meanwhile, place the tomatoes, cut-side up, with the chilli on a second baking tray, drizzle with 1 tablespoon of the olive oil and season. Bake for 10 minutes or until soft and coloured.

Heat the remaining 2 tablespoons of olive oil in a large saucepan over medium heat. Add the onion, garlic and ½ teaspoon sea salt. Cook for 10 minutes or until the onion is soft.

Add the roasted fennel, tomatoes, chilli and basil, and cover with stock. Bring to the boil, then process in a food processor or blender until smooth.

Return the soup to the pan, add the chickpeas and heat through. Ladle the soup into warm bowls, and finish with a drizzle of olive oil and freshly ground black pepper. Serve with crusty bread.

# PASTA E FAGIOLI

**SERVES 6**

*The classic Tuscan meal: half-soup, half-stew.
Full of beans and pasta, it hugs your ribs and
makes you feel warm inside and out. It should be
nice and thick - if it isn't, crush a few beans against
the side of the pan and stir them through for
instant, natural thickening.*

60 g (2¼ oz) butter or 3 tbsp olive oil

2 onions, finely chopped

2 carrots, finely chopped

3 celery stalks, finely chopped

6 roma (plum) tomatoes, peeled, seeded,
    finely chopped (or 400 g/14 oz tinned
    chopped tomatoes)

1 ham hock

1.5 litres (52 fl oz/6 cups) chicken stock

250 g (9 oz) podded peas

100 g (3½ oz) dried short macaroni or other
    short soup pasta

400 g (14 oz) cooked or tinned cannellini beans,
    rinsed, drained

¼ bunch each chervil, chives and flat-leaf
    parsley, leaves picked, chopped

parmesan, grated, to serve

crusty bread, to serve

Heat the butter or olive oil in a large saucepan over medium heat. Add the onion, carrot and celery and cook, stirring occasionally, for 10 minutes or until soft. Add the tomatoes and cook for 2 minutes, then add the ham hock and stock. Simmer gently for 2 hours.

Remove the ham hock from the soup, cool slightly, then shred the meat and discard the bone. Skim any excess fat off the soup.

Add the ham, peas and pasta to the soup and cook for 7 minutes or until the pasta is al dente and the peas are tender. Add the cannellini beans and heat through, then add the chervil, chives and parsley and season with sea salt and freshly ground black pepper.

Ladle the soup into warm bowls and serve with parmesan and crusty bread.

'Italians have always
known how to make
something very delicious
and nourishing out of
very little.'

# PARSNIP SOUP WITH GORGONZOLA

**SERVES 4**

*Italy does winter food so well, and this totally luxurious parsnip soup is proof in a bowl. Sweet, nutty root vegetables, blue cheese, new season walnuts... I love this.*

100 g (3½ oz) unsalted butter, chopped
1 onion, finely chopped
3 garlic cloves, finely sliced
6 parsnips, peeled, roughly chopped
200 ml (7 fl oz) thin (pouring) cream
1.5 litres (52 fl oz/6 cups) chicken or vegetable stock (Basics, 259)
100 g (3½ oz) gorgonzola
100 g (3½ oz) walnuts, toasted
olive oil, to serve
crusty bread, to serve

Melt the butter in a large saucepan over medium heat and add the onion, garlic and 1 teaspoon of sea salt. Cook for 10 minutes or until the onion is soft, without any colour.

Add the parsnip and cream, bring to the boil then reduce the heat to low and simmer until the cream is reduced by half. Add the stock, bring to the boil and simmer for 15 minutes or until the parsnip is soft.

Process in a food processor or blender until smooth and check the seasoning.

To serve, gently reheat the soup, ladle into warm bowls and crumble the gorgonzola and walnuts over the top. Finish with freshly ground black pepper and olive oil and serve with crusty bread.

# PAPPA AL POMODORO

**SERVES 6**

*Jamie Oliver says pappa al pomodoro is really good if you're very young or very old - as in, when you don't have any teeth - but people with teeth love it, too. This famous Florentine bread and tomato soup is really a way of using up overly ripe tomatoes and yesterday's bread. It's like drinking a fresh tomato sandwich. This is how we do it at Café Sopra, skinning the tomatoes and blending it to a smooth puree, but you can leave them unpeeled, rough and rustic if that's the way you roll.*

15 vine-ripened tomatoes (about 2 kg/4 lb 8 oz)

1/2 loaf day-old Italian-style bread

125 ml (4 fl oz/1/2 cup) extra virgin olive oil, plus extra to serve

8 garlic cloves, finely sliced

1 bunch basil, leaves picked, chopped

40 g (1 1/2 oz) parmesan, shaved

Bring a large saucepan of water to the boil. Cut a cross in the skin at the base of each tomato, and drop into the boiling water in batches, for 20 seconds or until the skin starts to peel away. Remove from the water and refresh immediately in a bowl of iced water. Discard the skins and cut the tomatoes in half. Scoop the seeds and juices into a bowl and set aside, then roughly chop the flesh.

Remove the crusts from the bread and discard, then tear the bread into 2 cm (3/4 in) chunks and set aside.

Heat the olive oil in a large saucepan over low heat, add the garlic and cook for 1 minute, without colouring, or until fragrant. Add the chopped tomatoes and basil, then strain the tomato seeds and juice over the mixture, bring to the boil and simmer for 15 minutes or until the tomatoes are pulpy.

For a smooth soup, process in a food processor or blender; otherwise, leave it nice and rustic.

To serve, gently reheat the soup and season with sea salt. Ladle the soup into warm bowls, scatter with the parmesan, drizzle with a little extra virgin olive oil, then grind over black pepper.

# MINESTRONE CON PESTO

**SERVES 6**

*Everyone seems to think this comforting family soup should be cooked until the vegetables are soft and sludgy and brown. We think if you have a vegetable soup, you have to be able to taste the vegetables. A massive dollop of pesto is crucial; it brings it all to life.*

1.5 litres (52 fl oz/6 cups) chicken or vegetable stock (Basics, 259)
1 bunch baby carrots, trimmed, peeled
2 celery stalks, trimmed, sliced
50 g (1¾ oz) cavolo nero, kale or cabbage, roughly chopped
100 g (3½ oz) podded peas (250 g/9 oz unpodded)
200 g (7 oz) baby green beans, trimmed
200 g (7 oz) kipfler potatoes, cooked, peeled, diced
200 g (7 oz) gnocchetti or similar small pasta, cooked
250 g (9 oz) cherry tomatoes
6 tbsp pesto (Basics, 255)
sliced crusty bread, to serve

To make the soup, bring the stock to the boil in a large saucepan. Add the carrots and celery and cook for 8 minutes or until tender. Add the cavolo nero, peas, beans and potatoes and cook for 3 minutes. Add the pasta and tomatoes, and heat through. Season with sea salt and freshly ground black pepper.

Ladle the soup into warm bowls and top with the pesto. Serve with crusty bread.

# FENNEL SOUP WITH SCALLOPS AND BASIL OIL

**SERVES 4**

*Nice flavours. Gentle. Everyone loves scallops, but the people who love the aniseedy taste of fennel as well are the lucky ones. If you don't like fennel, you miss out on a lot of beauty. This soup is luxurious but earthy, even without the scallops.*

100 g (3½ oz) unsalted butter, chopped
1 onion, chopped
4 garlic cloves, chopped
2 fennel bulbs, trimmed, sliced, fronds reserved
1.5 litres (52 fl oz/6 cups) fish or vegetable stock (Basics, 259)
2 tbsp light olive oil
12 fresh scallops, unsoaked
2 tbsp basil oil (Basics, 252)

In a large saucepan, melt the butter over medium heat. Add the onion and garlic with 1 teaspoon of sea salt and some freshly ground black pepper. Cook for 10 minutes or until the onion is translucent.

Add the sliced fennel and cook for a further 2 minutes, tossing well. Add the stock and bring to the boil, reduce the heat to low and simmer for 20 minutes or until the fennel is tender. Process in a food processor or blender until smooth. Check the seasoning.

Meanwhile, heat a frying pan until it starts to smoke, then add the olive oil. Season the scallops and cook for 1 minute on each side.

Ladle the soup into warm bowls and top with three scallops each. Drizzle with the basil oil, top with the reserved fennel fronds and serve.

TUNA CARPACCIO
PENADE & SHAVED BAB
VITELLO TONNAT

# il PRIMO

BITTER GREENS w POACHO
EGGS & ANCHOVY
PROSCIUTTO w ROASTED PEA
& BOCCONCINI
GRILLED KING PRAWNS w
TOMATO & BASIL w HO

# CRISP POLENTA WITH GORGONZOLA

**SERVES 6**

*We have customers who order this every single time they come to Café Sopra - and they're people who eat with us once, twice or three times a week. We can never, ever, ever take this off the menu or they will kill us. It's very rich, so it's a great dish to share.*

250 g (9 oz) fine polenta (cornmeal), plus extra
 for dusting
165 g (5¾ oz) butter, chopped
125 g (4½ oz) parmesan, finely grated
1 litre (35 fl oz/4 cups) thin (pouring) cream
150 g (5½ oz) gorgonzola dolce, crumbled
200 g (7 oz) button mushrooms, trimmed
100 g (3½ oz) swiss brown mushrooms, thickly sliced
olive oil, for deep-frying
¼ bunch flat-leaf parsley, leaves picked,
 chopped

To make the polenta, bring 1.5 litres (52 fl oz/6 cups) of water and 2 teaspoons of sea salt to the boil in a large heavy-based saucepan. Whisking continuously, add the polenta in a slow stream and continue to whisk for 10 minutes or until it begins to thicken. Reduce heat to low and cook, stirring frequently to prevent the mixture from catching on the base, for a further 30 minutes or until very thick.

Add 125 g (4½ oz) of the butter and the parmesan, stir until melted, then check the seasoning. Pour the polenta into an oiled 28 cm x 32 cm (11 in x 13 in) shallow tray, cool slightly, then refrigerate for 1 hour or until set.

Meanwhile, simmer the cream in a large saucepan over medium heat until reduced by half, then whisk in 100 g (3½ oz) of the gorgonzola until combined. Heat the remaining butter in a frying pan over medium-high heat. Add the button and swiss brown mushrooms and cook, tossing, for 5 minutes or until tender, then stir in the cream mixture and keep warm.

Turn out the polenta onto a chopping board and cut into 4 cm x 8 cm (1½ in x 3¼ in) rectangles (you should get 30-32). You can refrigerate the fingers for up to 2 days ahead if you like.

Fill a deep-fryer or large saucepan one-quarter full with olive oil and heat to 180°C (350°F).

Dust the polenta fingers with a little extra polenta, and shake off any excess. Fry the polenta, in batches of five, turning halfway through frying, until golden and crisp. Drain on paper towel.

To serve, stack the polenta fingers on each platter. Add the parsley to the cream mixture, spoon it over the polenta, scatter with the remaining gorgonzola and serve.

Note: This makes a lot but let's face it, you're going to need a lot.

# TUNA CARPACCIO WITH TAPENADE & SHAVED BABY FENNEL

## SERVES 4

*Fresh tuna is a surprisingly big flavour - it really is the steak of the sea - and black olive tapenade is one of the greatest, gutsiest condiments of the world. That's why you need something as fresh and light as the finely shaved fennel, with its amazing aniseed flavour.*

2 tbsp extra virgin olive oil
2 tbsp vegetable or light olive oil
1 tbsp lime juice
1 tbsp white wine vinegar
2 baby fennel bulbs, trimmed, halved
1 shallot, finely chopped
1 bunch chives, finely chopped
400 g (14 oz) sashimi-grade tuna, skinned, thinly sliced
1/2 lemon (optional)

### TAPENADE
150 g (5 1/2 oz) pitted kalamata olives
2 tsp salted baby capers, rinsed
2 anchovies in oil, drained
1/2 garlic clove, finely chopped
2 tbsp extra virgin olive oil

To make the tapenade, process all the ingredients in a food processor or blender until the mixture forms a paste, then transfer to a bowl and set aside.

To make the fennel salad, whisk together the oils, lime juice and vinegar in a bowl. Season with sea salt and freshly ground black pepper. Use a mandolin or sharp knife to shave the fennel, then toss with the shallot and chives, add the dressing and toss to combine.

Place the tuna slices between two sheets of plastic wrap, and use the flat side of a meat mallet or a rolling pin to gently pound until 2 mm (1/16 in) thick.

To serve, place a few slices of tuna on each plate and spread with the tapenade, leaving a 2 cm (3/4 in) border. Top with a pile of fennel salad and serve with the lemon half (if using).

# BITTER GREENS WITH POACHED EGG & ANCHOVY

## SERVES 4

*Salty, crunchy, sharp, bitter, sweet, creamy, warm and eggy - what's not to love? The bitter greens in question are beautiful, long-stemmed, green, leafy chicory (cicoria) - sort of like very wise, mature spinach that's full of character.*

2 bunches chicory (endive), stems trimmed
3 tbsp olive oil
pinch of chilli flakes
2 garlic cloves, finely chopped
finely grated zest and juice of 1 lemon
2 1/2 tbsp white vinegar
4 very fresh eggs

### ANCHOVY DRESSING
6 anchovies in oil, drained, finely chopped
1 sprig of rosemary, leaves picked, finely chopped
2 tbsp lemon vinaigrette (Basics, 254)

To make the dressing, whisk together the anchovies, rosemary and lemon vinaigrette.

Roughly chop the chicory. Heat the olive oil in a large saucepan or wok, add the chicory and cook, tossing for 5 minutes or until wilted. Add the chilli and garlic and cook for a further minute, then add the lemon zest and juice. Season to taste with sea salt and freshly ground black pepper.

Meanwhile, fill a large, deep saucepan with water and bring to a simmer, then add the vinegar. Break the eggs, one at a time into the water, and cook for 2 minutes or until the whites are set and the yolks are still runny. Use a slotted spoon to carefully remove the eggs from the water and drain on a clean tea towel (dish towel).

To serve, place the wilted chicory in the centre of each plate, top with a poached egg and scatter with a generous amount of the anchovy dressing.

# PROSCIUTTO WITH ROASTED PEAR & BOCCONCINI

**SERVES 4**

*This is how we serve a simple primo of prosciutto in winter, when pears are at their best. Bocconcini isn't poor man's mozzarella, by the way. It's often a better choice than buffalo mozzarella, especially when you want something that will hold its shape.*

2 corella pears, peeled
2 tbsp extra virgin olive oil, plus extra to serve
400 g (14 oz) prosciutto, very thinly sliced
200 g (7 oz) bocconcini (baby mozzarella), drained

Heat the oven to 180°C (350°F). Cut the pears into quarters and remove the core. Cut the quarters in half again lengthways. Place the pears in a roasting tin and drizzle with olive oil. Roast for 10 minutes, turning them halfway through, or until tender and golden. Remove from the oven and allow to cool to room temperature.

To serve, arrange the prosciutto on each plate. Top with the pears and the torn bocconcini. Drizzle with extra olive oil and scatter with freshly ground black pepper.

# BEEF CARPACCIO WITH CAPERS & ROCKET

**SERVES 4**

*It must be amazing for Arrigo Cipriani, the legendary owner of Venice's famous Harry's Bar, to see how this simple, simple dish invented by his father in 1950 has travelled around the world. This is our homage, made with the finest, freshest, most beautifully marbled beef that money can buy.*

500 g (1 lb 2 oz) wagyu beef fillet
1/2 lemon
100 g (3 1/2 oz) wild rocket (arugula)
40 g (1 1/2 oz) salted baby capers, rinsed
40 g (1 1/2 oz) parmesan, shaved
2 tbsp extra virgin olive oil

Cut the beef into 3 cm (1¼ in) thick pieces. Place each slice between two sheets of plastic wrap and gently pound with the flat side of a meat mallet or a rolling pin, until very thin.

To serve, arrange the beef in a single layer on each plate and season with sea salt and freshly ground black pepper.

Squeeze lemon juice over the top, and scatter with the rocket, capers and parmesan. To finish, drizzle with the extra virgin olive oil.

# GRILLED KING PRAWNS WITH ROAST TOMATO & BASIL BUTTER

**SERVES 4**

*People love prawns, and this is a really nice way of making those people happy. Besides, we're in Australia, surrounded by vast oceans. If we didn't have prawns on the menu, we'd have to be silly. This makes a lot of tomato and basil butter, so freeze it and use it when you want.*

250 g (9 oz) butter, at room temperature

50 g (1³/₄ oz) garlic confit (Basics, 253)

¹/₂ bunch basil, leaves picked, finely shredded

12 raw, unpeeled large king prawns (shrimp),
  cut in half lengthwise, deveined, tail intact

extra virgin olive oil, to serve

1 lemon, cut into wedges

### TOMATO JAM
**MAKES 200 g**

10 vine-ripened tomatoes, cored

4 tbsp olive oil

2 shallots, finely diced

1 garlic clove, crushed

splash of red wine vinegar

1 tsp sugar

Heat the oven to 150°C (300°F). To make the tomato jam, place the tomatoes in a roasting tin, drizzle with 2 tablespoons of the olive oil and roast for 1½ hours or until collapsed. In a frying pan, heat the remaining olive oil and sweat the shallots and garlic with some sea salt until soft. Pass the tomatoes through a mouli or coarse sieve into the pan with the shallots, add the vinegar and sugar, bring to a simmer and reduce to a jammy consistency. Check the seasoning, adding more sugar if necessary, and cool.

To make the butter, whisk the soft butter with electric beaters until very pale. Add 40 g (1½ oz) of the cooled tomato jam, the garlic confit and the basil, and season. Store the remaining tomato jam in an airtight container in the fridge for up to 5 days.

Heat a ridged cast-iron grill pan over high heat. Season the prawns and grill flesh-side down until nicely coloured. Turn over and grill briefly until just cooked through.

To serve, top the prawns with a large spoonful of the roast tomato and basil butter, drizzle with extra virgin olive oil and serve with lemon wedges.

# FRITTATA WITH ASPARAGUS & BLUE SWIMMER CRAB

SERVES 4

*This is another dish that has grown a cult of its own. Throwing it in the oven might sound unusual, but it really helps the frittata fluff up nicely. It's best served immediately it is ready.*

1¹/₂ tbsp lemon juice
4 tbsp extra virgin olive oil
16 asparagus spears, trimmed, halved
12 eggs
60 g (2¹/₄ oz) butter, chopped
100 g (3¹/₂ oz) cooked, picked blue swimmer crabmeat
sourdough toast, to serve

Whisk the lemon juice and olive oil together in a bowl, then season with sea salt and freshly ground black pepper and set aside.

Cook the asparagus in a saucepan of boiling water for 2-3 minutes or until almost tender. Drain, then refresh under cold running water and drain again.

Heat the oven to 200°C (400°F). Whisk three of the eggs in a large bowl, then season.

Heat one-quarter of the butter in an 18 cm (7 in) ovenproof frying pan. When foaming, add the whisked egg, then reduce heat to low. When it begins to set around the edges, use a spatula to pull the cooked edge towards the middle of the pan, allowing the uncooked mixture to run out onto the sides and under the frittata.

Cook for a further 2 minutes or until cooked around the edge but still soft in the middle. Slide the frittata onto a lightly greased baking tray, scatter with one-quarter of the crabmeat and asparagus, and transfer to the oven for a few minutes until set, but not coloured. Drizzle with a little of the lemon dressing and serve immediately with sourdough toast. Repeat with the remaining eggs, crabmeat and asparagus to make three more frittate.

# SALTED COD WITH MUSSELS

SERVES 4

*This is like a super-fresh, super-light version of baccala, the salted cod or stockfish that northern Italians adore.*

500 g (1lb 2 oz) blue eye trevalla or similar thick, white-fleshed fish, boned, skin removed
500 g (1 lb 2 oz) fresh mussels, scrubbed, bearded
100 g (3¹/₂ oz) unsalted butter
1 onion, diced
¹/₂ leek, pale part only, washed, finely sliced
2 garlic cloves, finely sliced
1 dutch cream potato, washed, peeled, cut into 1 cm (¹/₂ in) cubes
200 ml (7 fl oz) thickened (whipping) cream
4 eggs, freshly poached
juice of 1 lemon
100 ml (3¹/₂ fl oz) olive oil
¹/₄ bunch chives, chopped
4 slices ciabatta, toasted

Sprinkle 1 teaspoon of sea salt over the fish and refrigerate for at least 6 hours. Rinse the fish and dry on paper towel. Cut into 1 cm (¹/₂ in) cubes.

Discard any broken mussels, or opened ones that don't close when tapped on the bench. Place the mussels in a large, wide saucepan, cover and cook for 2-3 minutes, shaking the pan occasionally. Uncover the pan and remove the mussels with a slotted spoon as they open. Remove the meat and discard the shells. Set aside.

Melt the butter in a saucepan over medium heat and cook the onion, leek and garlic for 10 minutes. Add the potato and cream, bring to the boil, then reduce heat and simmer for 20 minutes or until the potatoes are tender.

Add the fish and cook for a further 5 minutes or until cooked through. Process in a food processor or blender until smooth, then cool to room temperature.

In a bowl, whisk together the lemon juice and olive oil, add the mussels and chopped chives and lightly toss.

To serve, place a toasted ciabatta slice on each plate, spoon a generous amount of salted cod pâté on top, add a poached egg and spoon the mussel mixture over.

# VITELLO TONNATO

**SERVES 6**

*Vitello tonnato is a summery, cold dish of veal in an amazingly more-ish tuna mayonnaise. There are a lot of very ordinary versions around town. For me, the veal has to be tender and finely sliced, and the flavour of the sauce has to have balance between richness, creaminess and acidity. This is terrific when you're having a few friends around for lunch; everyone can dig in and share, and it goes so well with a chilled glass of white.*

1 kg (2 lb 4 oz) veal shoulder
250 ml (9 fl oz/1 cup) white wine vinegar
220 g (7¾ oz) brown sugar
2 celery stalks, roughly chopped
1 carrot, roughly chopped
1 onion, roughly chopped
2 bay leaves
1 garlic bulb, halved
8 whole black peppercorns
thin slices of lemon, capers, chopped black olives, anchovies and chopped flat-leaf parsley leaves, to serve

### TUNA MAYONNAISE
160 g (5½ oz) tinned tuna in oil, drained
1 tbsp salted baby capers, rinsed
6 anchovies in oil, drained
juice of 1 lemon
500 ml (17 fl oz/2 cups) mayonnaise

Place the veal, vinegar, sugar, vegetables, bay leaves, garlic, peppercorns and 2 litres (70 fl oz/8 cups) of water in a large saucepan. Bring to the boil and simmer over low heat for 2½ hours or until the veal is tender. Remove from the heat and allow to cool to room temperature in the cooking liquid, then refrigerate overnight in the cooking liquid.

To make the tuna mayonnaise, whiz the tuna, capers, anchovies and lemon juice in a food processor or blender until smooth. Add the mayonnaise and process again, until smooth and well combined.

Remove the veal from its liquid and slice very finely. Layer a quarter of the slices in a ceramic dish or stainless steel tray, then spread less than a quarter of the tuna mayonnaise over the top. Repeat this layering three more times, covering the final layer of veal with a generous amount of the tuna mayonnaise. It can be made to this point a few hours ahead and kept refrigerated.

To serve, arrange lemon slices on top and scatter with capers, olives, anchovies and parsley.

# INGREDIENTI

Great Italian cooking depends on great Italian ingredients to give it that great Italian character and flavour dialect. The better the ingredients that go into it, no matter how simple and basic they may be, the better the food will taste. Along with the all-important salume and formaggi and, of course, pasta, which are covered elsewhere, these are the essentials, the building blocks, the fondazione, or foundation, of what makes Italian food Italian. Consider this your need-to-know guide.

## OLIO EXTRA VERGINE DI OLIVA

Extra virgin olive oil is the greatest oil in the world, bar none. It is the purest expression of the flavour of the olives, and of the region in which those olives were grown. The 'extra virgin' bit refers to oil produced by a simple pressing of the olives, leaving all its anti-oxidants and goodness intact. It's a fresh product, so store it away from direct heat and light, and use it generously and frequently. Other grades such as plain 'olive oil' use chemicals and heat to extract the oil, resulting in an industrial product. Try to keep a couple of different extra virgin olive oils in the kitchen, from light and spicy to dark and fruity.

## ACETO BALSAMICO

Balsamic vinegar is treated as a healing balsam in the elegant northern Italian town of Modena, where each noble family traditionally made their own prized vinegar. To make it, white trebbiano grapes are boiled down to a thick, sweet syrup known as saba. The mother vinegar is added and the vinegar matures in a series of barrels, each wood giving it a particular fragrance, colour and complexity. These vinegars can be aged 30 years or more and are labelled 'Aceto Balsamico Tradizionale di Modena'. They're worth saving up for, but there are also plenty of great balsamics aged for eight years or more that are great to use every day, in sauces, as dressings, over Parmigiano Reggiano, and even in certain cocktails that need a little lift.

## ACCIUGHE

A tin or jar of anchovy fillets preserved in olive oil is another essential ingredient, adding a power-packed salty punch to pizze and condimenti such as salsa verde and the creamy tuna sauce for vitello tonnato. Many Italians add a couple of anchovies to a slow-cooked stew or tomato sugo to give another layer of complexity. The marinated and pickled alici, or white anchovy, is a different kettle of fish altogether, so make sure you choose the right one for the recipe.

## FAGIOLE E LEGUME

Beans and pulses are an integral part of Italian cuisine. Pinkish, red-striped borlotti beans are available fresh, dried or canned. Cannellini beans, or white beans, should be soaked overnight if dried. Canned cannellini beans work well in salads, but can go slushy when cooked. Protein-rich lenticchie (lentils) are best purchased dried, and rinsed before cooking. If you're in a tearing hurry, you can buy them canned as well. The same with ceci (chickpeas). While grown mainly in the south, these wrinkled golden peas are popular throughout the country. Soak dried chickpeas overnight in cold water, then drain, cover in fresh cold water and simmer for 1 hour or until tender.

## CAPERI

The flower buds of a Mediterranean shrub, capers taste bitter when raw, and need to be cured in vinegar or brine, or dry-salted. Salted capers are the best for your pantry - the smaller the better - and will need a quick soak or rinse before use.

## TARTUFI

Although the famous white truffles of northern Italy are difficult to grow locally, the quality and availability of Australian cultivated black truffles (*Tuber melanosporum*) are getting better and better. In season in July and August, they are best and most aromatic finely shaved or grated over warm egg dishes, pasta and risotto.

## HERBS

Our chefs couldn't move without mountains of aromatic herbs at their fingertips. You wouldn't believe how much basil, rosemary, oregano and parsley (the European flat-leaf variety, not the curly stuff) they go through. Fresh is always best, although we do also have a soft spot for dried oregano.

## RISO

Rice for risotto is different from normal supermarket rice, jasmine or basmati, in that it has short, plump grains, which release their starch over long, slow cooking to give risotto its characteristically creamy texture. The three varieties we use are grown in the Po Valley in the north of Italy: arborio, vialone and carnaroli. Our favourite is the carnaroli, which has a higher starch content and firmer texture, and tends to keep its shape better during cooking.

## POLENTA

Polenta is a term used for both the ingredient - yellow cornmeal, or ground maize - and the finished dish, a glorious golden 'porridge'. Traditional polenta must be cooked long and slow while stirring continuously. Instant polenta, pre-cooked, dried and re-milled, is a good product and very useful as well. You can serve it 'soft' and runny, or allow it to set and then cut into shapes to grill, bake or fry.

## TOMATO PASSATA

Tomato passata is a cooked tomato sauce 'passed' through a sieve so that it is smooth, not to be confused with tomato paste (conserva di pomodoro), which is a concentrated puree. To make your own quick tomato passata or sugo, cook a can of chopped tomatoes with a glug of olive oil, a handful of capers, another handful of basil leaves, a finely sliced garlic clove and a dash of water. Simmer for 15 minutes, and use as a simple pasta sauce, add to soups and braises, or spoon over vegetables such as zucchini.

*'Extra virgin olive oil is the purest expression of the flavour of the olives, and of the region in which those olives were grown.'*

ENNE ALLA PUTTANES
HA RAGU AL BOLOGNE
PASTA
INE W LEMON

# FRESH PASTA

**MAKES 1 QUANTITY (SERVES 4)**

*You know the drill. The biggest pot in the house, please. Lots of water, lots of salt. If you forget to salt the water, the pasta will taste bland, and no amount of salt added later will make it taste any better. That said, by all means reduce the salt a bit if you are serving a very salty sauce with anchovies and capers.*

*Add the pasta to the boiling water and give it a minute or so to come back to the boil, then stir, so it doesn't stick together. Don't add any olive oil as some people tell you - it's a waste of good olive oil. Then it's up to you how al dente you like your pasta. It should be tender, yet still firm to the bite, or the teeth, which is what al dente means.*

*But it's not just a matter of boiling the pasta until it's tender enough to eat; it's actually more about boiling it enough to get it to the point where it releases its starch - then it's ready to eat.*

*If you had an Italian grandmother, she would advise you to save a little of the starchy, salty cooking water when you drain the pasta, and use it to help loosen the sauce and fuse the pasta and sauce together. (I don't do this myself, though, because I don't particularly like the taste of the pasta water, and I'm not an Italian grandmother.)*

*She would also recommend using the right shape of pasta for the sauce, and I agree with her there. I love serving orecchiette with a slow-cooked ragu, for instance - it's like having lots of little spoons to pick up the sauce. And penne with a bolognese sauce, because the sauce gets trapped inside the pasta.*

*That said, I know people who will eat anything as long as it comes with spaghetti. Here's how to make your own pasta; something I recommend doing if you can't get a table at Café Sopra.*

400 g (14 oz) '00' flour, plus extra for dusting
4 eggs (60 g/2¼ oz each)
drizzle of olive oil

To make the pasta, form a mound of the flour and a pinch of sea salt, then make a crater in the centre, big enough to take the eggs. Break the eggs into the hole, add a drizzle of olive oil (about 1 tablespoon) and get in there with your fingers, breaking it all up. Gradually draw in a little flour, then a little more, until you have one unholy mess of eggy flour. Perfect. Just keep going, and you will soon have a rough dough you can form into a ball.

Or you can simply place the flour, sea salt, eggs and olive oil in a food processor and pulse until it forms a large clump. Tip onto a lightly floured work surface and bring the mixture together with your hands.

Knead the dough for 10 minutes or until smooth and elastic. If it feels a little dry, wet your hands with water and continue to knead. If it feels a little sticky, then flour your hands and continue to knead.

Wrap the dough in plastic wrap and rest for 1 hour.

Set up your pasta machine with the machine rollers at their widest mark, flour your bench, and you're ready.

Cut the dough into four pieces. Flatten out one piece with your hands or with a rolling pin, and feed it through the machine. Feed it through twice more on the same setting, then continue the process, changing the setting one notch and feeding it through once each time until you have long, fine sheets. You can dust the pasta with a little flour if it starts to get too soft during the process.

For agnolotti and ravioli, continue as per recipe. For tagliatelle, feed the pasta through the cutting attachment on the machine and hang to dry. For pappardelle, cut the pasta with a knife into long strips 2 cm (¾ in) or 3 cm (1¼ in) wide. For lasagne, cut by hand into squares 10 cm x 10 cm (4 in x 4 in). Once dry, lightly dust the pasta with semolina or flour, and store in a cool place until ready to use.

# ORECCHIETTE WITH CALAMARI & PISTACHIO PESTO

**SERVES 4**

*The good thing about this dish is you can slow-cook the tomatoes and make the pistachio pesto ahead of time (and have plenty of both left over for the next day's cooking as well), whereas the calamari itself takes just seconds.*

250 g (9 oz) orecchiette, gnocchetti or small pasta
2 tbsp vegetable oil
300 g (10$^1/_2$ oz) cleaned calamari (squid), tubes and tentacles
handful rocket (arugula) leaves, torn
2$^1/_2$ tbsp lemon vinaigrette (Basics, 254)
extra virgin olive oil, to serve

**SLOW-COOKED TOMATOES**
200 g (7 oz) grape tomatoes
4 tbsp extra virgin olive oil
1$^1/_2$ tbsp balsamic vinegar
handful torn basil leaves

**PISTACHIO PESTO**
125 g (4$^1/_2$ oz) pistachio nuts
2 garlic cloves
4 anchovies in oil, drained
1 tbsp salted baby capers, rinsed
pinch of chilli flakes
small handful flat-leaf parsley leaves, chopped
4 tbsp extra virgin olive oil
lemon juice, to taste

To make the pistachio pesto, use a mortar and pestle to pound the nuts, garlic, anchovies, capers and chilli until you have a fine paste. Mix through the parsley, olive oil, and some lemon juice and sea salt to taste.

To slow-cook the tomatoes, heat the oven to 120°C (250°F). Combine the tomatoes, olive oil, vinegar and basil in an ovenproof dish that will fit the tomatoes snugly. Season with sea salt and freshly ground black pepper and bake for up to 1 hour or until the tomatoes are tender but still intact.

Cook the orecchiette in boiling, salted water until al dente, then drain.

To cook the calamari, heat the vegetable oil in a frying pan over high heat and sauté the calamari with a pinch of sea salt for 20 seconds. Add 2 tablespoons of the pesto to the pan with the tomatoes and 2 tablespoons of their liquid and toss through to warm up. Remove from the heat and add the drained orecchiette, rocket and lemon vinaigrette.

Check the seasoning and finish with a drizzle of extra virgin olive oil.

Store the remaining pesto in an airtight jar in the fridge for up to 3 days.

# RIGATONI WITH WILD BOAR RAGU

**SERVES 4**

*Wild boar, known to the Italians as cinghiale, is a gamier, leaner version of pork, with great flavour. You'll find it at good butchers and Italian food specialists.*

100 ml (3½ fl oz) olive oil

1 kg (2 lb 4 oz) wild boar shoulder, cut into 1 cm (½ in) cubes

1 onion, finely chopped

6 garlic cloves, finely chopped

1 bunch oregano, leaves chopped

2 bay leaves

500 ml (17 fl oz/2 cups) red wine

1 litre (35 fl oz/4 cups) chicken stock

400 g (14 oz) tinned chopped tomatoes

300 g (10½ oz) rigatoni or penne

100 g (3½ oz) parmesan, grated

Heat the olive oil in a large saucepan over medium heat. Add the wild boar and cook for 5 minutes or until brown all over.

Remove from the pan and set aside. Add the onion, garlic, oregano and bay leaves to the pan and cook for 10 minutes or until soft. Add the wine, bring to the boil and reduce until nearly dry. Return the meat to the pan with the stock and tomatoes and simmer over very low heat, uncovered, for 2½-3 hours or until the meat is very tender. Check seasoning.

Meanwhile, cook the rigatoni in a large saucepan of boiling, salted water until al dente, then drain.

Toss the rigatoni through the sauce and divide among pasta bowls. Scatter with the parmesan and serve.

# PASTA RAGU
# AL BOLOGNESE

**SERVES 4**

*Aaah, spag bol. Or tag bol, or penne bol. This is the sort of dish you don't mess around with. We try to keep it a constant in every restaurant, so that it tastes exactly the same whether you have it before the theatre at Walsh Bay Café Sopra or after work at Café Sopra Potts Point. When I make it at home, I often add a dash of balsamic vinegar towards the end of cooking.*

100 ml (3½ fl oz) olive oil
1 onion, finely chopped
3 garlic cloves, finely sliced
1 tsp chilli flakes
500 g (1lb 2 oz) minced (ground) veal
200 ml (7 fl oz) thin (pouring) cream
200 ml (7 fl oz) tomato passata
300 g (10½ oz) pasta
¼ bunch mint, leaves chopped
100 g (3½ oz) parmesan, grated

To make the bolognese sauce, heat the olive oil in a large saucepan over medium heat. Add the onion, garlic, chilli and 1 teaspoon of sea salt and cook for 10 minutes or until soft.

Add the veal a little at a time to break up any lumps, stirring well, until all the veal is nicely browned.

Add the cream and simmer for 20 minutes or until almost completely reduced.

Add the passata and cook over very low heat for 30 minutes or until the fat rises to the top. Skim off the fat and discard.

Cook the pasta in a large saucepan of boiling, salted water until al dente, then drain. Add to the sauce with the mint - ideally, use just enough sauce to coat the pasta rather than drown it. Taste for seasoning, and serve with grated parmesan.

# AGNOLOTTI OF VEAL, SAGE & PROSCIUTTO

**SERVES 4**

*With all that flavour trapped inside the little pasta packets, the sauce outside can be as simple as melted butter and sage. You can freeze the uncooked agnolotti immediately on making them, then transfer them straight from the freezer into the boiling water if you like.*

2 x 200 g (7 oz) veal and chicken sausages
200 g (7 oz) veal tenderloin, roughly chopped
100 g (3½ oz) prosciutto, finely chopped
80 g (2¾ oz) parmesan, grated, plus extra to serve
2 eggs, lightly whisked (in separate bowls)
1 quantity fresh pasta (page 85), in sheets
200 g (7 oz) butter, chopped
½ bunch sage leaves, picked

Heat the oven to 180°C (350°F). Heat a heavy-based frying pan over medium heat. Skin the sausages and crumble the meat into the pan. Add the veal and cook for 5 minutes, turning, until browned and cooked through, then set aside to cool.

Combine the cooled meat, prosciutto, parmesan and one of the whisked eggs in a food processor until it forms a coarse paste. Season well and refrigerate until needed.

Halve the pasta sheets lengthwise, and place teaspoons of the filling along one sheet, 5 cm (2 in) apart, in two rows. Brush the pasta with the remaining whisked egg, then place the remaining half pasta sheet on top to enclose filling. Press between the fillings to remove air pockets, then use a pastry wheel or knife to cut into small squares. Layer on a tray between sheets of baking paper. Repeat with the remaining pasta and filling.

Cook the agnolotti in a large saucepan of boiling, salted water for 2 minutes or until they float to the surface. Drain, season well and divide between pasta bowls.

Working quickly, melt the butter in a small frying pan over medium heat, add the sage and cook for 1 minute or until crisp. Spoon over the agnolotti, scatter with extra grated parmesan and serve.

# PENNE ALLA PUTTANESCA

SERVES 4

*The old story is that this sauce was thrown together in a hurry from easily available ingredients by the street girls of Naples, who had very little time between 'clients' to make something to eat. It's still the best choice for any working girl - or bloke - with very little time.*

30 kalamata olives
4 tbsp extra virgin olive oil
1/2 fresh long red chilli, finely sliced, seeded, plus extra to serve
4 garlic cloves, very finely sliced
6 anchovies in oil, drained
500 ml (17 fl oz/2 cups) tomato passata
2 tbsp salted baby capers, rinsed
400 g (14 oz) penne

Use the heel of your palm to flatten the olives, one at a time, then tear open, discard the pit and tear the olives in half again.

Place the olive oil, chilli, garlic and anchovies in a deep frying pan and stir over low-medium heat until the garlic is pale golden and the anchovies have melted.

Add the passata and simmer for 5 minutes, stirring occasionally. Add the olives and capers and heat through.

Cook the penne in a large saucepan of boiling, salted water until al dente. Drain, then add to the tomato sauce and toss until well coated.

Divide among pasta bowls and scatter with the extra chilli.

# CASARECCIA AL FORNO WITH SILVERBEET

SERVES 4

*If it's called al forno, it's baked in the oven. This is a great way of getting pasta lovers to eat their greens. You can use silverbeet, kale or cavolo nero but not spinach, which is too delicate for the oven baking.*

1 bunch silverbeet (Swiss chard), washed
100 g (3½ oz) butter
4 garlic cloves, finely sliced
2 large flat mushrooms, sliced
300 g (10½ oz) casareccia
500 ml (17 fl oz/2 cups) thickened (whipping) cream
100 g (3½ oz) parmesan, grated

Heat the oven to 220°C (425°F). Separate the stalks and leaves of the silverbeet, and roughly shred both, keeping leaves and stalks separate.

Melt the butter in a large saucepan over medium heat. Cook the garlic for 5 minutes or until soft and fragrant but not coloured. Add the mushrooms and cook for 5 minutes or until tender.

Cook the casareccia in a large saucepan of boiling, salted water or until al dente, then drain.

Add the silverbeet stalks to the mushrooms, and cook for 2 minutes. Add the cream and simmer for 10 minutes or until the sauce is thick enough to coat a spoon. Fold in the silverbeet leaves, pasta, sea salt and freshly ground black pepper, transfer to a baking dish, and top with the parmesan.

Bake for 10 minutes or until golden on top, then serve.

# ORECCHIETTE ALLA PRIMAVERA

**SERVES 4**

*You can always tell when spring has sprung, because this pasta comes out of hibernation, with all the joy of young, new-season broad beans and spinach.*

600 g (1 lb 5 oz) unpodded broad (fava) beans
300 g (10½ oz) cooked or tinned cannellini beans, rinsed, drained
1 garlic clove, finely chopped
juice of 1½ lemons
100 ml (3½ fl oz) olive oil
400 g (14 oz) orecchiette
200 g (7 oz) peas, podded
8 baby artichoke hearts preserved in olive oil, drained, halved
100 g (3½ oz) baby English spinach leaves
2 tbsp grated pecorino

Pod the broad beans and cook in a small saucepan of boiling, salted water for 2 minutes. Remove, cool under running water and 'double-peel', slipping off the skins to reveal the pretty inner green bean.

Process the cannellini beans, garlic, lemon juice and olive oil in a food processor until smooth, then transfer to a large frying pan.

Cook the orecchiette in a large saucepan of boiling, salted water until al dente, then drain, reserving 250 ml (9 fl oz/1 cup) of cooking water.

Add the reserved water to the cannellini bean puree, stirring. Add the broad beans, peas and artichokes and cook over medium heat for 2-3 minutes or until the vegetables are just tender. Add the orecchiette and spinach, and toss until the pasta is hot and the spinach is wilted.

Divide among pasta bowls, scatter with the pecorino and serve.

# LINGUINE WITH LEMON, CHILLI, GARLIC & PANGRATTATO

**SERVES 4**

*With such a simple dish, everything has to be perfect. The quality of the olive oil is super-important, it really shines through and pulls together the lemony, garlicky flavours; and the pangrattato (effectively, crunchy breadcrumbs) gives the whole thing texture. It's also popular with prawns, so feel free.*

200 g (7 oz) day-old Italian-style bread
150 ml (5 fl oz) extra virgin olive oil
2 lemons
4 garlic cloves, finely chopped
400 g (14 oz) linguine
1 cup (30 g/1 oz) finely chopped flat-leaf parsley
½ tsp chilli flakes

Heat the oven to 190°C (375°F). To make the pangrattato, remove the crusts from the bread, then tear the bread into coarse breadcrumbs. Place the breadcrumbs on a small baking tray, season with sea salt and freshly ground black pepper, drizzle with 1 tablespoon of the olive oil, then toss to coat. Bake for 10-12 minutes or until golden, then remove and cool.

Finely grate the lemon zest and place in a bowl, then juice the lemons into the bowl. Add the remaining olive oil and the garlic and whisk to combine.

Cook the linguine in boiling, salted water until al dente, then drain. Toss with the parsley, chilli, lemon dressing and half the pangrattato.

Divide among pasta bowls and serve with the remaining pangrattato.

# MEATBALLS WITH BUCATINI AND RICH TOMATO SAUCE

**SERVES 6**

*We think the meatballs are more important than the sauce and the pasta, so that's how we write it on the blackboard; meatballs first. This is based on a recipe from the brilliant Janni Kyritsis, a generous chef and friend. It's everybody's favourite; people get cross if we've already sold out.*

60 g (2¼ oz) butter, chopped
2 onions, finely chopped
3 garlic cloves, finely chopped
½ tsp each chilli flakes, ground cumin
   and ground nutmeg
¼ tsp ground cloves
1 kg (2 lb 4 oz) minced (ground) veal
½ bunch mint, chopped
½ bunch flat-leaf parsley, chopped, plus extra to serve
3 eggs, lightly whisked
150 ml (5 fl oz) thin (pouring) cream
150 g (5½ oz) dry breadcrumbs
50 g (1¾ oz) parmesan, grated, plus extra to serve
3 tbsp olive oil
375 g (13 oz) bucatini or spaghetti

**RICH TOMATO SAUCE**

2 tbsp olive oil
60 g (2¼ oz) butter, chopped
2 onions, finely chopped
3 garlic cloves, finely chopped
800 g (1 lb 12 oz) tinned chopped tomatoes
200 ml (7 fl oz) tomato passata
½ teaspoon dried chilli flakes

To make the rich tomato sauce, heat the olive oil and butter in a saucepan over medium heat. Add the onion and garlic and cook for 10 minutes or until softened. Add the tomatoes, passata and chilli and cook over low-medium heat for 45 minutes or until thickened.

To make the meatballs, heat the butter in a frying pan over medium heat, add the onion and garlic, and cook, stirring occasionally, for 10 minutes or until soft. Stir in the spices, transfer to a large bowl and allow to cool.

Add the veal, 2 teaspoons of sea salt, herbs, eggs, cream, breadcrumbs and parmesan to the onion mixture, mixing well with your hands to combine. Shape into 100 g (3½ oz) balls.

Heat the olive oil in a frying pan over medium heat, add half the balls and cook, turning occasionally, for 5 minutes or until evenly browned. Repeat with the remaining balls. Heat the oven to 200°C (400°F). Place the meatballs in a large ovenproof dish, pour over the tomato sauce, cover with foil and bake for 45 minutes or until cooked through.

Cook the bucatini in a large saucepan of boiling, salted water until al dente, then drain. To serve, top the bucatini with the meatballs and sauce, and scatter with extra parsley and parmesan.

# GNOCCHETTI WITH SCALLOPS & SALSA VERDE

**SERVES 4**

*Here's a trap for young players - gnocchetti isn't gnocchi at all, but pasta. They're short little curves of dried pasta from Sardinia that look like ridged little bugs. I think of this as luxury fast food, because you can throw it together in a jiffy.*

400 g (14 oz) gnocchetti or similar small pasta
400 g (14 oz) fresh sea scallops, unsoaked
3 tbsp olive oil
juice of 1 lemon

**SALSA VERDE**
50 g (1³⁄₄ oz) salted baby capers, rinsed
60 g (2¹⁄₄ oz) anchovies in oil, drained
2 garlic cloves, chopped
2 tsp dijon mustard
185 ml (6 fl oz/³⁄₄ cup) extra virgin olive oil
1 bunch flat-leaf parsley, leaves picked

To make the salsa verde, combine all ingredients except the parsley in a food processor and process until you have a coarse paste. Add the parsley and whiz again to a paste.

Cook the gnocchetti in a large saucepan of boiling, salted water until al dente, then drain.

Cut the scallops in half if large, and season. Heat a frying pan over high heat until smoking, add the olive oil and sear the scallops for 20 seconds on each side or until just cooked.

Transfer to a bowl and combine with the gnocchetti, 5 tablespoons of the salsa verde and lemon juice to taste.

Divide among pasta bowls and serve immediately.

# GNOCCHI WITH MUSHROOMS & TALEGGIO

**SERVES 4**

*This is a great dish for vegetarians and anyone who loves mushrooms. The onion and garlic give the whole thing a complexity that adds depth and sweetness.*

2¹⁄₂ tbsp olive oil
¹⁄₂ onion, finely chopped
2 garlic cloves, finely chopped
4 large flat mushrooms, peeled, sliced
1 quantity gnocchi, cooked (Basics, 254)
3 tbsp chopped flat-leaf parsley
juice of ¹⁄₂ lemon
150 g (5¹⁄₂ oz) taleggio, rind removed, chopped
50 g (1³⁄₄ oz) parmesan, finely grated

Heat the oven to 220°C (425°F).

Heat the olive oil in a frying pan over medium heat, and cook the onion and garlic for 5 minutes or until tender but not coloured.

Add the mushrooms and cook, tossing occasionally, for 8 minutes or until tender.

Add the cooked gnocchi, parsley, lemon juice and taleggio to the mushrooms and gently fold through, being careful not to break the gnocchi.

Transfer to an ovenproof dish, scatter with the parmesan and bake for 10 minutes or until golden and the taleggio has melted. Spoon into pasta bowls and serve immediately.

# GNOCCHI ALLA ROMANA WITH SALSA NAPOLETANA

**SERVES 4–6**

*Gnocchi alla romana is different from potato gnocchi, because it's made with semolina. In that sense, it has more in common with polenta, making a beautifully tender, light baked dish that is then cut into circles or triangles, overlapped on a bed of simple, fresh tomato sauce, topped with mozzarella and baked until light and fluffy.*

1.5 litres (52 fl oz/6 cups) milk
375 g (13 oz) fine semolina
200 g (7 oz) parmesan, grated
150 g (5¹⁄₂ oz) butter, chopped
3 eggs
¼ bunch each chives and flat-leaf parsley
2 x 250 g (9 oz) balls buffalo mozzarella, drained

**SALSA NAPOLETANA**
1 tbsp olive oil
1 tbsp butter, chopped
1 onion, finely chopped
2 garlic cloves, finely chopped
400 g (14 oz) tinned chopped tomatoes
500 g (1 lb 2 oz) roma (plum) tomatoes, peeled, seeded, finely chopped
100 ml (3¹⁄₂ fl oz) tomato passata
1 tsp chilli flakes
1 bunch basil, leaves picked, torn

To make the salsa napoletana, heat the olive oil and butter in a saucepan over medium heat. Add the onion and garlic and cook for 10 minutes or until tender. Add the tinned and fresh tomatoes, passata, chilli and 1 teaspoon of sea salt, and simmer gently for 30 minutes or until thickened. Stir in the basil and check the seasoning.

Lightly oil a shallow tray approximately 28 cm x 48 cm (11 ¼ in x 19 in) (or two smaller ones).

To make the gnocchi, place the milk in a large heavy-based saucepan and bring almost to the boil over medium heat. Reduce heat to low. Whisking slowly and continuously, pour the semolina in a steady stream into the milk, then add 2 teaspoons of sea salt and stir until thickened.

Swap to a wooden spoon and stir continuously for 5 minutes or until the mixture is thick enough for the spoon to stand upright on its own.

Remove from the heat and stir in all except 1 tablespoon of the parmesan, then the butter, eggs and herbs. Spoon the mixture into the oiled tray and refrigerate for 1½ hours.

Heat the oven to 220°C (425°F). Spoon the salsa napoletana into a lightly oiled ovenproof dish. Use a floured round or crescent-shaped pastry cutter to cut the semolina, and overlap them in rows on the sauce. Tear the buffalo mozzarella into pieces and scatter over the top, scatter with the remaining parmesan, and bake for 6 minutes or until golden. Serve immediately.

# BRAISED LAMB NECK WITH ORECCHIETTE & LENTILS

**SERVES 4**

*My daughter Grace and I had something similar to this dish at Del Posto in New York and loved it. They have fabulous wines by the glass, with different vintages of Italy's great varietals. I don't know how I did it, but I managed to pick up my first glass of (red) wine and pour it all over my (white) shirt. Tip: Ask your butcher to split the lamb neck in half. And don't wear a white shirt.*

100 ml (3½ fl oz) olive oil, plus extra to serve
500 g (1 lb 2 oz) lamb neck, on the bone, split in half
2 tbsp plain (all-purpose) flour, seasoned
1 onion, finely chopped
3 garlic cloves, finely sliced
1 tbsp thyme sprigs
1 bay leaf
250 ml (9 fl oz/1 cup) white wine
500 ml (17 fl oz/2 cups) chicken stock
250 g (9 oz) orecchiette
200 g (7 oz) peas, podded
250 g (9 oz/1 cup) cooked lentils
4 tbsp chopped flat-leaf parsley

**CARROTS**
2 carrots, cut in half
500 ml (17 fl oz/2 cups) orange juice
50 g (1¾ oz) caster (superfine) sugar

To cook the carrots, combine the carrots, orange juice, sugar and 500 ml (17 fl oz/2 cups) of water in a small saucepan and cover with a round of baking paper. Bring to the boil, then simmer very gently for 2 hours or until very soft, removing the paper halfway through. Cool, drain, roughly chop and set aside.

Heat the oven to 150°C (300°F). Heat the olive oil in a large frying pan. Dust the lamb neck in flour, shaking off any excess, and fry for 5 minutes or until browned all over. Transfer to a small roasting tin.

In the same pan, cook the onion, garlic, thyme, bay leaf and 1 teaspoon of sea salt for 10 minutes or until soft. Add the wine, bring to the boil and reduce until almost completely evaporated. Add the stock and return to the boil.

When the stock comes to the boil, pour it over the lamb neck and cover with foil. Bake for 3-3½ hours or until the meat is falling off the bone. Remove the meat from the liquid and set aside. Transfer the stock back to the stovetop and bring back to the boil. Simmer until reduced by half.

Cook the orecchiette in a large saucepan of boiling, salted water until al dente, then drain.

Shred the lamb off the bones and return the lamb to the reduced sauce. Add the peas and simmer for 5 minutes or until tender. Add the drained orecchiette, lentils and carrots and check the seasoning.

To serve, divide among pasta bowls and top with parsley and a drizzle of olive oil.

# PENNE WITH GREEN BEANS, POTATOES & PESTO

**SERVES 4**

*We use baby potatoes for this dish because their skin is so thin you don't need to peel them - and because most of the nutritional goodness of a potato is just under the skin.*

**8 baby potatoes**
**20 green beans, topped but not tailed**
**300 g (10½ oz) penne**
**2 tbsp olive oil**
**4 tbsp pesto (Basics, 255)**
**drizzle of lemon vinaigrette (Basics, 254)**

Cook the potatoes for 15 minutes or until tender, remove from the water, then cook the beans for 3 minutes or until tender, then drain. Cook the pasta in a large saucepan of boiling, salted water until al dente, then drain.

Cut the potatoes into quarters. Heat the olive oil in a frying pan and fry the potatoes for 5 minutes or until golden all over. Transfer to a warm bowl, and add the pasta, pesto, beans and lemon vinaigrette.

Toss well to combine and taste for seasoning. Divide among pasta bowls and serve immediately.

# LAMB RAGU WITH PENNE, CHILLI & ROSEMARY

**SERVES 4**

*This is another dish we can't take off the menu. There are people who come to Café Sopra just to have the lamb ragu. It's a beautiful sauce, very rich. We always serve it with a short pasta such as penne, tubetti or orecchiette, never a long pasta.*

1 kg (2 lb 4 oz) lamb shoulder, boneless, cut into 1 cm (1/2 in) dice
800 ml (28 fl oz) tomato passata
2 tsp chilli flakes
1/2 bunch rosemary, leaves picked
6 anchovies in oil, drained
200 g (7 oz) penne
40 g (11/2 oz) parmesan, grated

Heat the oven to 160°C (315°F). Heat a frying pan over medium heat until it just starts to smoke. Season the lamb and fry the meat in batches until well browned. Transfer to a deep roasting tin.

Bring the passata, chilli, rosemary and anchovies to the boil in a saucepan over medium heat. Pour the sauce over the lamb and cover tightly with foil, and a lid, too, if possible.

Bake for 3 hours or until the lamb is tender, then taste for seasoning.

Meanwhile, cook the penne in a large saucepan of boiling, salted water until al dente, then drain. Toss through the lamb ragu.

To serve, divide among pasta bowls and top with the parmesan.

*'There are rules and laws for everything in Italy. Especially pasta.'*

# TAGLIATELLE WITH FRESH BLACK TRUFFLE & PARMIGIANO

## SERVES 4

*Butter, truffle and parmesan, oh yeah. Italian truffles are wonderful, pungent and earthy, but Australia now has a healthy truffle industry of its own, with the 'black gold' harvested from June to August. Don't wash your truffle, just brush it with a clean toothbrush to dislodge any grit, and shave it over the top of hot, buttery, cheesy pasta at the last minute, to release that beautiful aroma.*

400 g (14 oz) tagliatelle
100 g (3½ oz) unsalted butter
100 g (3½ oz) Parmigiano Reggiano, grated
40 g (1½ oz) fresh black truffle

Cook the tagliatelle in a large saucepan of boiling, salted water until al dente, then drain and place in a warm bowl.

Melt the butter in a small saucepan over low heat then add to the tagliatelle with 1 teaspoon of sea salt, freshly ground black pepper, and half the parmesan, tossing well.

Shave half the truffle over the top, using a truffle slice or mandolin, and toss well. Divide among pasta bowls, and take to the table.

Shave the remaining truffle over the top at the table and scatter with freshly ground black pepper and the remaining parmesan.

# SPAGHETTI ALLA CARBONARA

**SERVES 4**

*One of the greats. A rich egg and bacon sauce, with cheese thrown in for added fun. Lots of people add cream to their carbonara, which is so not Italian - but if you want, go ahead. Either way, make sure you toss the pasta and egg together while it's still super-hot, so that the egg cooks into its famously creamy, cheesy sauce.*

**400 g (14 oz) spaghetti**
**4 eggs**
**4 egg yolks**
**80 g (2³/4 oz) parmesan, grated**
**200 g (7 oz) finely sliced pancetta or bacon**
**2 tsp olive oil**
**15 g (¹/2 oz/³/4 cup) flat-leaf parsley leaves, roughly chopped**

Cook the spaghetti in a large saucepan of boiling, salted water until al dente.

Meanwhile, whisk together the eggs and yolks in a large bowl. Add the parmesan and sea salt and freshly ground black pepper, then set aside.

Cut the pancetta into matchsticks. Heat the olive oil in a frying pan over medium heat and cook the pancetta, tossing well, until crisp. Remove with a slotted spoon and drain on paper towel.

As soon as the spaghetti is cooked, drain and quickly toss with the egg mixture, pancetta and parsley until well coated. Divide among pasta bowls and serve immediately.

# CASARECCIA WITH RICOTTA & ZUCCHINI FLOWERS

**SERVES 4**

*Zucchini's bright and beautiful tangerine-coloured flowers are a delicate and beautiful addition to pasta in their own right. Any short tubular pasta is good here, such as penne or rigatoni.*

**3 tbsp extra virgin olive oil, plus extra to serve**
**2 garlic cloves, finely sliced**
**500 g (1 lb 2 oz) cherry tomatoes, halved**
**400 g (14 oz) casareccia**
**200 g (7 oz) fresh ricotta**
**200 g (7 oz) male zucchini (courgette) flowers, stems removed, petals torn**
**handful baby basil leaves**

Heat the olive oil in a large frying pan over medium heat, add the garlic and cook for 3 minutes or until soft and fragrant but not coloured.

Add the tomatoes and 1 teaspoon of sea salt and cook for 6 minutes or until the tomatoes have blistered and are starting to soften.

Meanwhile, cook the casareccia in a large saucepan of boiling, salted water until al dente. Drain, then toss the casareccia through the tomato mixture. Add the ricotta, zucchini flowers and half the basil, tossing well.

Divide among pasta bowls and top with freshly ground black pepper, a drizzle of olive oil and the remaining basil.

# TAGLIATELLE WITH SALSICCE & PEAS

## SERVES 4

*Now here's a good trick. Buy really good-quality sausages, peel off the skin and turn the insides into instant meatballs.*

1 tbsp butter
1 small onion, finely chopped
3 lamb and rosemary sausages, or similar
2 tbsp finely chopped mint leaves
250 g (9 oz) tagliatelle
250 g (9 oz) fresh podded peas or frozen peas
juice of 1 lemon
125 g (4$^{1}/_{2}$ oz) mascarpone
2 tbsp olive oil
40 g (1$^{1}/_{2}$ oz) pecorino, finely grated

Heat the butter in a frying pan over medium heat, add the onion and cook for 5 minutes until soft, then cool.

Squeeze the meat from the sausage casings into a bowl, discarding the casings. Add the cooked onion and the mint, mixing well. Using your hands, form the mixture into 2.5 cm (1 in) meatballs.

Cook the tagliatelle in a large saucepan of boiling, salted water until al dente, then drain, reserving 3 tablespoons of the cooking water.

Cook the peas in a small saucepan of boiling, salted water for 3 minutes or until tender, then drain well. Return the peas to the pan and crush lightly with a fork. Add the lemon juice and mascarpone and season with sea salt and freshly ground black pepper.

Heat half the olive oil in a frying pan, add the meatballs and cook on all sides for 4 minutes or until brown and cooked through. Add the pasta, pea mixture, reserved water and remaining olive oil, then season and toss over medium heat until hot.

To serve, divide the tagliatelle, meatballs and sauce among pasta bowls and top with grated pecorino.

# LASAGNE AL FORNO

## SERVES 4

*This is Italian comfort food, good and proper. It's all about generosity and hospitality, so make heaps.*

200 g (7 oz) parmesan, grated
good $^{1}/_{2}$ bunch basil, leaves chopped
1 quantity bolognese sauce (page 89)
10 sheets fresh pasta (page 85), or 10 dried lasagne sheets, cooked

### BECHAMEL SAUCE
50 g (1$^{3}/_{4}$ oz) unsalted butter, chopped
50 g (1$^{3}/_{4}$ oz) plain (all-purpose) flour
500 ml (17 fl oz/2 cups) milk

To make the bechamel, melt the butter in a saucepan over low heat. As soon as it has melted, add the flour all at once, and cook gently for 10 minutes, stirring constantly to stop it from colouring. Add the milk 100 ml (3$^{1}/_{2}$ fl oz) at a time, stirring constantly and letting it all combine before adding the next 100 ml. When all the milk is added, season with 1 teaspoon of sea salt and cook for a further 5 minutes.

Add half the bechamel, three-quarters of the parmesan and all the basil to the bolognese sauce and stir well to combine.

Heat the oven to 180°C (350°F). In a lightly oiled 20 cm (8 in) square roasting tin or equivalent, spoon a thin layer of bolognese sauce on the bottom. Cover with a layer of pasta, and continue layering until all the pasta is used (five layers).

Pour the remaining bechamel over the top of the final layer of pasta, and scatter with the remaining parmesan. Bake for 30 minutes or until a knife goes through the pasta easily, and the top is golden. Cut into squares and serve.

# PAPPARDELLE WITH DUCK RAGU

**SERVES 4**

*These lovely thick, flat ribbons of fresh egg pasta love a rich duck or wild boar (cinghiale) ragu. If making your own fresh pasta, cut it into 3 cm (1¼ in) wide ribbons with a knife. If you have dried pappardelle, follow the recipe as is.*

2 cooked duck marylands (confit or roasted)
100 ml (3½ fl oz) olive oil
100 g (3½ oz) flat pancetta, cut into batons
½ onion, finely chopped
3 garlic cloves, finely chopped
1 small carrot, finely chopped
1 celery stalk, finely chopped
400 g (14 oz) tinned chopped tomatoes
250 ml (9 fl oz/1 cup) chicken stock
2 tbsp chopped sage leaves
400 g (14 oz) fresh pappardelle
grated parmesan, to serve

Pick the meat and skin off the cooked duck, discarding the bones, and roughly shred.

Heat the olive oil in a large saucepan over medium heat. Add the pancetta and cook for 5 minutes or until crisp. Then add the onion, garlic, carrot, celery and sea salt to taste, and cook for 10 minutes or until soft. Add the shredded duck and the tomatoes and cook for 20 minutes or until thickened. Add the stock and simmer for a further 10 minutes, then add the sage and check the seasoning.

Cook the pappardelle in a large saucepan of boiling, salted water until al dente, then drain. To serve, toss the pappardelle through the ragu and divide among pasta bowls.

Top with parmesan and freshly ground black pepper and serve.

# RISOTTO

**SERVES 4**

*It's easy. Pour a glass of your favourite Italian wine and put it by the stove. Start cooking the onions until the whole kitchen smells sweet. Take a sip of your wine. Coat the rice grains in the buttery onions, and take another sip. Slow down your movements, get into the swing of it. Make sure your stock is ready, kept on a gentle simmer where it is easy to reach.*

*Add wine (not yours) to the rice and let it almost boil away. It's going to a good home - giving the risotto complexity while evaporating the alcohol content. The main focus of your attention is to add the hot stock a ladleful at a time, adjusting the heat under the pan so that it just mooches along, neither too high nor too low, allowing you to stir calmly and serenely with your wooden spoon, taking the occasional sip of wine.*

*You can almost feel your body temperature calming, your mind focusing. You are in the meditative Zen zone of risotto cooking. And the lucky people who eat your risotto will know it has been cooked by a happy cook, rather than by someone rushing to get dinner on the table or angry about having to cook dinner instead of eating out.*

*By the time you have finished your glass of wine - about 20 minutes, give or take the odd re-fill - your risotto will be ready for you and you will be ready for it. Northern Italians have the best way of describing how your risotto should be when it is perfectly cooked - all'onda - in the manner of a wave, meaning it would move slowly like an ocean wave if you tilted the plate.*

1.5 litres (52 fl oz/6 cups) vegetable (Basics, 259) or chicken stock
2 tbsp extra virgin olive oil
2 tbsp butter, chopped
1 onion, finely diced
2 garlic cloves, crushed
300 g (10 1/2 oz) arborio or carnaroli rice, unwashed
200 ml (7 fl oz) white wine
2 tbsp grated parmesan

Heat the stock and keep it at a gentle simmer. Heat the oil and half the butter in a heavy saucepan over medium heat, and cook the onion and garlic with 1 teaspoon of sea salt for 10 minutes or until the onion is soft.

Add the rice and cook for 2 minutes, stirring until well coated. Add the wine, bring to the boil and simmer, stirring, until reduced by half. Add the hot stock a ladleful at a time, stirring continuously, adding the next ladleful when the previous one has been absorbed.

Continue to add enough stock to keep the rice wet, while allowing it to slowly absorb and cook in the heat of the liquid - this should take about 20 minutes. When the rice is just tender, add the parmesan and remaining butter, beating well. Serve on warm dinner plates.

## 'By the time you have finished your glass of wine, the risotto will be ready.'

# RISOTTO
# WITH OXTAIL
**SERVES 4**

*Risotto and red wine? Definitely. If you're adding slow-braised meaty goodness such as an oxtail ragu, then use a red wine in the risotto instead of white, and you'll get a beautifully rich risotto that is a red-wine magnet in itself.*

1.5 litres (52 fl oz/6 cups) chicken or vegetable stock (Basics, 259)
2 tbsp extra virgin olive oil
2 tbsp butter, chopped
1 onion, finely diced
2 garlic cloves, crushed or finely chopped
300 g (10½ oz) arborio or carnaroli rice, unwashed
300 ml (10½ fl oz) red wine
100 g (3½ oz) parmesan, grated
1 tbsp lemon juice

### OXTAIL RAGU
2 tbsp olive oil
1.5 kg (3 lb 5 oz) oxtail pieces
1 onion, finely sliced
2 garlic cloves, finely sliced
1 celery stalk, finely sliced
500 ml (17 fl oz/2 cups) red wine
1 litre (35 fl oz/4 cups) beef or chicken stock
2 tbsp thyme sprigs

To make the ragu, heat the olive oil in a large saucepan over medium heat. Season the oxtail and fry for 5 minutes on each side until browned. Remove and set aside. Add the onion, garlic and celery and cook for 10 minutes or until tender. Add the wine, bring to the boil and cook until reduced by half.

Return the oxtail to the pan, add the stock and the thyme, bring to the boil and simmer gently for 3½ hours or until the meat falls off the bone. Remove from the liquid and cool slightly. Shred the meat from the bone and set aside.

To make the risotto, heat the stock and keep it at a gentle simmer. Heat the oil and half the butter in a heavy saucepan over medium heat and cook the onion and garlic with 1 teaspoon of sea salt for 10 minutes or until the onion is soft.

Add the rice and cook for 2 minutes, stirring until well coated. Add the wine, bring to the boil and simmer, stirring, until reduced by half. Add the hot stock a ladleful at a time, stirring continuously, adding the next ladleful when the previous one has been absorbed. When the rice is just tender - about 20 minutes - fold in the meat, and beat in the remaining butter, parmesan and lemon juice. Serve on warm dinner plates.

# RISOTTO WITH BITTER GREENS

**SERVES 4**

*Chicory (cicoria) is a long, slightly bitter vegetable with divided dark-green leaves, found at farmer's markets and in good greengrocers such as, well, Fratelli Fresh. Or use any bitter greens such as cavolo nero, kale or dandelion greens.*

1.5 litres (52 fl oz/6 cups) chicken or vegetable stock (Basics, 259)
1/2 bunch chicory, roughly chopped
2 tbsp butter, chopped
1 onion, finely diced
2 garlic cloves, crushed or finely chopped
300 g (10 1/2 oz) arborio or carnaroli rice, unwashed
250 ml (9 fl oz/1 cup) red wine
2 tbsp grated parmesan
2 tbsp grated pecorino
1 tbsp lemon juice

Heat the stock and keep it at a gentle simmer. In a saucepan of boiling, salted water, blanch the chicory for 2 minutes or until wilted and the stalks are tender. Drain, squeeze dry and finely chop. Melt half the butter in a heavy saucepan. Add the onion, garlic and 1 teaspoon of sea salt and cook for 10 minutes or until tender. Add the rice and cook for 2 minutes, stirring until well coated. Add the wine, bring to the boil and simmer, stirring, until reduced by half. Add the hot stock a ladleful at a time, stirring continuously, adding the next ladleful when the previous one has been absorbed. When the rice is just tender - about 20 minutes - fold in the chicory, and beat in the remaining butter, parmesan, pecorino and lemon juice. Serve on warm dinner plates.

# RISOTTO AI FUNGI WITH TALEGGIO

**SERVES 4**

*If you're cooking this for vegetarians, use a vegetable stock - we have a good recipe in Basics, 259. Feel free to mix up the types of mushrooms according to what's around. Marsala is a fortified wine from Sicily, well worth having to hand.*

1.5 litres (52 fl oz/6 cups) chicken or vegetable stock (Basics, 259)
1 large flat mushroom
50 g (1 3/4 oz) button mushrooms
50 g (1 3/4 oz) swiss brown mushrooms
2 tbsp extra virgin olive oil
2 tbsp butter, chopped
1 onion, finely diced
2 garlic cloves, crushed or finely chopped
300 g (10 1/2 oz) arborio or carnaroli rice, unwashed
250 ml (9 fl oz/1 cup) white wine
2 tbsp Marsala
100 g (3 1/2 oz) taleggio, grated
100 g (3 1/2 oz) parmesan, grated
1 tbsp lemon juice
2 tbsp finely chopped flat-leaf parsley

Heat the stock and keep it at a gentle simmer. Slice the flat mushroom, button mushrooms and swiss brown mushrooms. Heat the olive oil and half the butter in a heavy saucepan over medium heat, and cook the onion and garlic with 1 teaspoon of sea salt for 10 minutes or until the onion is soft. Add the rice and the sliced mushrooms and cook for 2 minutes, stirring until well coated. Add the wine and Marsala, bring to the boil and simmer, stirring, until reduced by half. Add the hot stock, a ladleful at a time, stirring continuously, adding the next ladleful when the previous one has been absorbed. When the rice is just tender - about 20 minutes - beat in the remaining butter, taleggio, parmesan, lemon juice and parsley. Serve on warm dinner plates.

# RISOTTO WITH ARTICHOKES & BROAD BEANS

**SERVES 4**

*This beautiful spring/summer risotto is light, fresh and green. Globe artichokes have an amazing flavour that gets taken up by the rice and cries out for lots of Parmigiano.*

2 globe artichokes
200 ml (7 fl oz) white wine
200 ml (7 fl oz) white wine vinegar
3 tbsp brown sugar
100 g (3½ oz) podded broad (fava) beans
1.5 litres (52 fl oz/6 cups) chicken or vegetable stock (Basics, 259)
2 tbsp extra virgin olive oil
2 tbsp butter, chopped
1 onion, finely diced
2 garlic cloves, crushed or finely chopped
300 g (10½ oz) arborio or carnaroli rice, unwashed
250 ml (9 fl oz/1 cup) white wine
2 tbsp grated parmesan
2 tbsp grated pecorino
1 tbsp lemon juice

Trim the artichokes by pulling off and discarding the rough outer leaves. Cut each artichoke into quarters and remove the inner furry bits. Cut in half again.

Combine the artichokes with 400 ml (14 fl oz) of water, the wine, vinegar and sugar in a non-reactive saucepan and bring to the boil. Simmer for 20 minutes or until tender, then drain and set aside.

Cook the broad beans in a saucepan of simmering, salted water for 2 minutes. Drain, discard the outer skins and set aside.

To make the risotto, heat the stock and keep it at a gentle simmer. Heat the oil and half the butter in a heavy saucepan over medium heat. Add the onion, garlic and 1 teaspoon of sea salt and cook for 10 minutes or until tender. Add the rice and cook for 2 minutes, stirring until well coated. Add the wine, bring to the boil and simmer until reduced by half. Add the hot stock, a ladleful at a time, stirring continuously, adding the next ladleful when the previous one has been absorbed. When the rice is just tender - about 20 minutes - fold in the broad beans and the artichokes, and beat in the remaining butter, parmesan, pecorino and lemon juice. Serve on warm dinner plates.

...no bruschetta v pesto

Fritto Misto Di Pesce

Chicken Cacciatore

il Secondo

...esce All'Acqua Pazza

...rmesan-Crumbed Chicken

...timbocca v Spinac &

# BISTECCA FIORENTINA

**SERVES 2**

*Sometimes you just have to have a great steak, hand-cut chips, salad leaves with a sharp vinaigrette (see the radicchio side on page 171) and a glass of red. With this legendary Tuscan classic, you cannot get away with anything but the best-quality meat. We use a Poll Hereford from NSW, using the t-bone cut off the short loin, complete with bone. It's important to take the steak out of the fridge and leave, covered, at room temperature for at least an hour, to raise its internal temperature.*

4 kipfler potatoes, scrubbed
2 tbsp olive oil
1 kg (2 lb 4 oz) t-bone steak
2 tbsp salsa verde (Basics, 256)

Heat the oven to 220°C (425°F). Cook the potatoes in boiling, salted water until almost tender. Drain and cut lengthways into quarters. Toss the potatoes in olive oil and sea salt and bake for 30 minutes or until golden brown, shaking occasionally.

Meanwhile, heat a barbecue, charcoal grill or a ridged cast-iron chargrill pan. Season the meat well with sea salt and freshly ground black pepper and place on the grill. Cook for 3 minutes, then turn 90 degrees to get cross-hatched grill marks.

Cook for a further 3 minutes and turn. Repeat after a further 3 minutes then place the steak in the lower part of the oven for 10 minutes. Turn the steak, and cook for another 10 minutes.

When cooked to your liking (we recommend medium-rare), remove from the oven and rest, covered, for 10 minutes.

Serve on the bone, or cut the meat off the bone into slices, and serve with the roast potatoes and salsa verde.

# ROAST PORK BELLY WITH ROSEMARY POLENTA

**SERVES 4**

*At the restaurant, we often serve a thick wedge of pork belly on its own, without polenta or sauce, so people can really get stuck into the crunchy crackling and the sweet, tender, milky meat. Here, rosemary polenta, a crisp apple salad and a side of broccolini with anchovy crumbs (see page 171) turn it into a magnificent meal.*

1 kg (2 lb 4 oz) piece pork belly, skin on, boned
2 tbsp olive oil
1 apple (eg gala), finely sliced
1/2 bunch rocket (arugula)
1 lemon, cut into wedges

**ROSEMARY POLENTA**
50 g (1³/₄ oz) butter
1 bunch rosemary, leaves finely chopped
100 g (3¹/₂ oz) instant polenta (cornmeal)
50 g (1³/₄ oz) parmesan, grated
plain (all-purpose) flour, for dusting

To make the polenta, melt the butter in a small saucepan over low heat. Add the rosemary and infuse for 5 minutes, being careful not to colour the butter.

In a separate saucepan, bring 600 ml (21 fl oz) of water to the boil over medium heat, and slowly pour in the polenta, whisking continuously. When the polenta comes back to the boil, reduce the heat to low and simmer, stirring, for 3-4 minutes (it will be extremely hot and may start to spit, so be careful). Add the rosemary butter and parmesan, pour into an oiled tray and refrigerate for 1 hour or until cool.

Heat the oven to 220°C (425°F). Place the pork on a chopping board and use a sharp knife to score the skin at 1 cm (¹/₂ in) intervals, cutting just through the skin.

Place in a roasting tin skin-side up and rub the skin with 1 tablespoon of sea salt. Roast for 1 hour or until the skin has crackled, then reduce the oven temperature to 180°C (350°F) and roast for another 1¹/₂ hours. Remove from the oven and rest in a warm place for 30 minutes.

Cut the polenta into 7.5 cm (3 in) squares, then cut diagonally. Dust with flour and shake off any excess. In a frying pan, heat half the olive oil over medium heat and fry the polenta for 3 minutes on each side or until golden.

Core and finely slice the apple and toss with the rocket and the remaining olive oil. Cut thick slices of pork belly and serve with the polenta, apple salad and a lemon wedge.

# FEGATO ALLA VENEZIANA

**SERVES 4**

*The Venetians have always served calves' liver with sweet, slow-cooked onions as a contrast to the rich, livery quality of the meat. Ask your butcher to trim the calves' liver for you and to slice it as finely as they can.*

125 g (4½ oz) unsalted butter
3 onions, sliced 5 mm (¼ in) thick
3 garlic cloves, finely sliced
1 bunch sage, chopped, plus extra to serve
2 tbsp extra virgin olive oil
750 g (1 lb 10 oz) fresh calves' liver, finely sliced

Melt the butter in a heavy-based frying pan over medium heat. Add the onion, garlic and a good pinch of sea salt and cook over low heat, stirring constantly, until the onion turns translucent - it must remain pale.

When it is soft, and starts to catch on the bottom of the pan, add the sage, toss well and remove from the heat.

Heat the olive oil in a separate frying pan. Once hot, season the strips of liver and fry for 30 seconds over high heat, then flip over and cook for another 30 seconds - do this in batches or it will stew and not fry. Keep the livers pink in the middle, and keep the cooked livers warm while you cook the remaining livers.

Serve the livers with the onion and a few extra sage leaves.

# CHICKEN CACCIATORE

**SERVES 4**

*In the old days, when people didn't know much about Italian regional food, this was the dish they did know - a simple, beautiful stew of 'hunter's chicken'. It's good served with soft polenta (Basics, 258) or mashed potato; in fact, very good.*

2–3 tbsp olive oil

4 chicken Marylands (leg quarters), thighs and legs separated

1 onion, finely chopped

1/2 tsp chilli flakes

2 garlic cloves, sliced

250 ml (9 fl oz/1 cup) white wine

6 roma (plum) tomatoes, chopped

400 g (14 oz) tinned chopped tomatoes

20 g (3/4 oz) black olives, pitted, roughly chopped

3 tbsp roughly chopped flat-leaf parsley

In a large saucepan, heat the olive oil over medium heat. Cook the chicken for 5 minutes on each side or until golden and set aside.

Add the onion, chilli and garlic to the pan and cook for 10 minutes or until soft. Add the wine, bring to the boil and reduce until almost completely evaporated. Add the fresh and tinned tomatoes with 200 ml (7 fl oz) of water and bring to the boil. Return the chicken to the saucepan and cover with baking paper. Simmer for 45-50 minutes or until the chicken is tender. Add the olives and parsley and serve with soft polenta or mashed potato.

# BRAISED BEEF CHEEKS WITH SOFT POLENTA

**SERVES 4**

*This is a cold-night dish, full of beautifully gelatinous meat, earthy mushrooms, pancetta and plenty of sauce to go with the soft, golden polenta.*

50 g (1¾ oz) plain (all-purpose) flour
4 x 280 g (10 oz) beef cheeks, trimmed
110 ml (3½ fl oz) olive oil
1 onion, roughly chopped
4 garlic cloves, roughly chopped
1 carrot, roughly chopped
2 celery stalks, roughly chopped
½ bunch thyme, leaves picked
2 bay leaves
250 ml (9 fl oz/1 cup) red wine
1 litre (35 fl oz/4 cups) chicken or beef stock
100 g (3½ oz) pancetta, cut into batons
2 large flat mushrooms, sliced
¼ bunch flat-leaf parsley, leaves chopped
soft polenta (Basics, 258)

To cook the beef, season the flour with sea salt and freshly ground black pepper. Coat the beef in the flour and shake off any excess. Heat 3 tablespoons of the olive oil in a large ovenproof cast-iron pan over medium heat. Fry the beef for 5 minutes on each side or until browned, then remove and set aside. Add a further 1 tablespoon of the olive oil to the pan and cook the onion, garlic, carrot, celery, thyme and bay leaves for 10 minutes or until they start to soften. Add the wine, bring to the boil and simmer until almost completely evaporated. Add the stock and bring back to the boil. Return the beef to the pan and simmer, partly covered, for 3½-4 hours or until very tender.

Remove the meat, vegetables and herbs, and strain the sauce through a fine sieve. Bring the sauce back to the boil and simmer until reduced by one-third.

Heat the remaining olive oil over medium heat. Add the pancetta and cook until crisp. Add the mushrooms and cook for a further 5 minutes or until tender. Add the sauce, the beef cheeks and parsley and gently heat through.

To serve, spoon the hot, soft polenta into shallow bowls and arrange the beef and the sauce on top.

# FRITTO MISTO DI PESCE

**SERVES 4**

*Fritto misto means mixed fry, and pesce means fish, so this couldn't be simpler - fresh fish and prawns dipped in a light batter and deep-fried until crunchy and golden. Serve with grilled marinated vegetables (see page 170).*

vegetable oil, for deep-frying
1/2 bunch mint, leaves chopped
1/2 bunch marjoram, leaves chopped
8 large king prawns (shrimp), peeled, deveined with tail intact
4 x 60 g (2 1/4 oz) flathead fillets or similar white-fleshed fish fillets
4 x 60 g (2 1/4 oz) salmon or ocean trout pieces
4 calamari (squid) cleaned, tentacles reserved
2 lemons, cut into wedges
200 g (7 oz) aioli (Basics, 252)

**BATTER**
200 g (7 oz) plain (all-purpose) flour
450 ml (16 fl oz) chilled sparkling water

To make the batter, place the flour and 1 teaspoon of sea salt in a bowl. Whisk the sparkling water into the flour until it coats your finger when you dip it in. Refrigerate for 30 minutes.

Heat the oil in a deep-fryer or deep saucepan to 180°C (350°F). Whisk the herbs into the batter.

Working in batches, dip the prawns into the batter, allowing the excess batter to run back into the bowl, then lower them into the hot oil and fry for 3 minutes. Drain the prawns on paper towel and repeat with the fish, cooking for 3 minutes, then the calamari and tentacles, cooking for 2 minutes.

Drain and serve immediately, with sea salt, lemon wedges and aioli.

# ZUPPA DI PESCE

**SERVES 4**

*Prawns, squid and fish (there are some suggestions here, but pretty much any fish from tuna to swordfish to snapper to salmon) along with mussels and clams all combine in a very happy and tomato-y celebration of the sea. Make a special trip to a great fishmonger or fish market and get messy at the table - it's the only way to really enjoy it.*

400 g (14 oz) black mussels, scrubbed, bearded
400 g (14 oz) clams (vongole)
250 ml (9 fl oz/1 cup) dry white wine
140 ml (4¾ fl oz) olive oil, plus extra to serve
2 onions, finely chopped
2 garlic cloves, finely sliced
pinch of chilli flakes
500 g (1 lb 2 oz) roma (plum) tomatoes, chopped
250 ml (9 fl oz/1 cup) tomato passata
200 g (7 oz) salmon fillet, pin-boned
200 g (7 oz) barramundi fillet, pin-boned
8 large raw prawns (shrimp), deveined with tail intact
400 g (14 oz) calamari (squid) cleaned, sliced,
  tentacles reserved
2 tbsp gremolata (Basics, 255)
warm crusty bread, to serve

Discard any broken mussels, or opened ones that don't close when tapped on the bench. Place the mussels, clams and wine in a wide saucepan, then cover and cook over medium heat for 3-5 minutes, shaking the pan occasionally, until just opened. Strain through a fine sieve, reserving the cooking liquid.

Heat 100 ml (3½ fl oz) of the olive oil in a large saucepan over medium heat and cook the onion and garlic for 5 minutes or until tender. Add the chilli and tomatoes and cook for 5 minutes or until the tomatoes are pulpy. Add the passata and reserved cooking liquid and simmer for 5 minutes or until slightly thickened.

Meanwhile, cut the fish fillets into four pieces each and season. Heat the remaining oil in a frying pan over medium-high heat and cook the seafood in batches, about 1 minute each side for the fish and the prawns, and 30 seconds each side for the squid.

Transfer the seafood to a large casserole or serving dish and add the clams and mussels. Stir the gremolata through the broth and pour over the seafood, drizzle with olive oil and serve with warm crusty bread.

*'An endlessly changing pot of small miracles that can use up any sort of fish and seafood you may have.'*

# BRAISED SQUID WITH PEAS & POTATOES

**SERVES 6**

*The thing about squid or calamari is that you have to cook it for a long time or a short time. Cook it fast, and it's tender. Keep cooking it, and it's tough. But keep on cooking it, and it gets tender again.*

1 kg (2 lb 4 oz) calamari (squid), cleaned
1.5 kg (3 lb 5 oz) vine-ripened tomatoes
500 g (1 lb 2 oz) kipfler potatoes
100 ml (3½ fl oz) olive oil, plus extra to serve
2 large red (Spanish) onions, finely chopped
1 bunch flat-leaf parsley (leaves and stalks), chopped
200 g (7 oz) podded peas
crusty bread, to serve

Cut the calamari into 1 cm (½ in) rings, reserving the tentacles. Peel, seed and chop the tomatoes. Peel and roughly chop the potatoes.

Heat the olive oil in a large ovenproof cast-iron pan over medium heat. Add the onion, season with sea salt and freshly ground black pepper and cook for 10 minutes or until soft.

Add the calamari rings and tentacles, tomatoes and 100 ml (3½ fl oz) of water and simmer for 45 minutes or until the squid is almost tender. Add the potatoes and parsley and simmer for a further 30 minutes or until the potatoes are tender. Add the peas and simmer for a further 5 minutes or until tender. Divide among bowls or dinner plates and serve with a drizzle of olive oil and crusty bread.

# RABBIT IN BRODO WITH PARSNIPS

**SERVES 4**

*This is nonna food, the sort of dish a grandmother would make to bring the whole family together at the table. The parsnips and leeks add a beautiful vegetable sweetness to the broth.*

75 g (2¾ oz) butter, chopped
5 celery stalks, finely chopped
2 onions, finely chopped
2 garlic cloves, finely sliced
1 tsp chilli flakes
3 anchovies in oil, drained, chopped
250 ml (9 fl oz/1 cup) dry white wine
1 litre (35 fl oz/4 cups) chicken stock
1.6 kg – 1.8 kg (3 lb 8 oz – 4 lb) farmed white rabbit, jointed
75 g (2¾ oz) plain (all-purpose) flour, seasoned
2 tbsp olive oil
1 bunch baby carrots, trimmed
3 small parsnips
1 bunch baby (pencil) leeks or 1 small leek, pale part only
100 g (3½ oz) baby English spinach

Heat the oven to 150°C (300°F). Melt the butter in a large casserole dish over low-medium heat. Add the celery, onion, garlic, chilli, anchovies and 1 tablespoon of sea salt and cook, stirring occasionally, for 5 minutes or until the vegetables are soft. Add the wine and simmer until almost evaporated. Add the stock and bring to the boil.

Meanwhile, dust the rabbit with the flour, and shake off the excess.

Heat the olive oil in a frying pan over medium heat and brown the rabbit in batches on both sides, then add to the casserole. Return to the boil and cover with a lid or seal with foil, then transfer to the oven and bake for 30 minutes.

Peel the carrots and parsnips. Cut the carrots in half or on the diagonal if large. Cut the parsnips into rough baton shapes. Trim the baby leeks to 15 cm (6 in) and cut on the diagonal or, for a normal leek, trim, cut in half then cut on the diagonal.

Add the vegetables (except for the spinach) to the casserole dish after the first 30 minutes of cooking, and cook for a further 30 minutes or until the rabbit is cooked through and the vegetables are tender.

Add the baby spinach until softly wilted, check seasoning, and serve.

# PESCE ALL' ACQUA PAZZA

**SERVES 4**

*This literally means 'fish in crazy water', because apparently the local southern Italian fishermen were crazy enough to cook the smaller of their catch in sea water while still out at sea. Use snapper, blue eye trevalla or any firm, white-fleshed, cod-like fish.*

100 ml (3$\frac{1}{2}$ fl oz) olive oil
4 x 180 g (6$\frac{1}{2}$ oz) white-fleshed fish fillets,
  pin-boned
handful basil leaves
handful flat-leaf parsley leaves
1 tbsp picked chervil leaves
2 tbsp lemon juice

**ACQUA PAZZA SAUCE**
3 tbsp extra virgin olive oil
4 garlic cloves, finely sliced
good pinch of chilli flakes
8 roma (plum) tomatoes, cut into 2 cm ($\frac{3}{4}$ in) chunks
good handful basil leaves
1 tsp caster (superfine) sugar
juice of $\frac{1}{2}$ lemon

To make the sauce, heat the olive oil in a large frying pan. Add the garlic, chilli and 1 teaspoon of sea salt and cook gently for 3 minutes or until lightly golden. Add the tomatoes and 150 ml (5 fl oz) of water, cover and bring to the boil. Remove from the heat, remove lid and add the basil, sugar and lemon juice. Check for seasoning.

To cook the fish, heat the oven to 220°C (425°F). Heat all except 1 tablespoon of the olive oil in an ovenproof frying pan. Season the fish and add to the pan, skin-side down.

Cook for 1 minute, then put the pan in the oven for 5 minutes or until just cooked through.

Toss the herbs in a bowl with the lemon juice, sea salt, freshly ground black pepper and remaining olive oil.

To serve, divide the acqua pazza sauce between shallow bowls, place the fish and the herb salad on top.

# COTECHINO WITH LENTILS & SALSA VERDE

**SERVES 4**

*Cotechini are large, soft, plump sausages that are a combination of pork, pork rind and pork fat spiced with cinnamon, cloves and pepper. They are the sausages all other sausages want to be when they grow up. To prepare a fresh, uncooked cotechino, prick the sausage all over with a very fine skewer, wrap it snugly in muslin (cheesecloth) and place in a large saucepan of cold water. Bring to the boil, then reduce the heat to a gentle simmer and cook for 2 hours. Cool and unwrap.*

1 kg (2 lb 4 oz) dried lentils (Puy or Castelluccio)
1 onion, quartered
1 large carrot, diced
2 celery stalks, sliced
1 bunch thyme sprigs
2 x 500 g (1 lb 2 oz) vacuum-packed cotechino
4 tbsp salsa verde (Basics, 256)

Cover the lentils in twice their volume of water and leave to soak overnight, then drain.

Fill a large saucepan with 3 litres (105 fl oz/12 cups) of cold water. Add the lentils, onion, carrot, celery and thyme. Bring to the boil, then simmer for 20 minutes or until tender. Drain and cool the lentils.

Place the vacuum-packed cotechini in a saucepan of boiling water and simmer for 20 minutes or as instructed. Remove, discard the packaging and thickly slice.

To serve, spoon the lentils into shallow bowls, and arrange the cotechino and salsa verde on top. Serve immediately.

# PARMESAN-CRUMBED CHICKEN

## SERVES 4

*Good old scallopini, it never goes out of style. Serve this golden-crumbed chicken with a pile of Café Sopra slaw (see page 170) - it's a real crowd-pleaser.*

2 x 250 g (9 oz) skinless chicken breast fillets, tenderloin removed
100 g (3½ oz) plain (all-purpose) flour
4 eggs, lightly whisked
100 ml (3½ fl oz) milk
440 g (15½ oz) fine dry breadcrumbs
100 g (3½ oz) parmesan, grated, plus extra to serve
100 g (3½ oz) butter
100 ml (3½ fl oz) olive oil
1 lemon, cut into wedges

Place 1 chicken fillet on a chopping board. Hold a knife parallel with the board and cut the breast in half, going from the thick end to the thin end. Place the half-breast between two sheets of baking paper and lightly tap with a meat mallet until an even thickness. Repeat with the remaining chicken fillet.

Place the flour, the combined eggs and milk, and the combined breadcrumbs and parmesan in three separate bowls. Lightly dust one piece of chicken with the flour, then dip into the egg mix, then place it on the crumb mix and cover with crumbs, lightly pressing the crumbs into the chicken. Dip the chicken back into the egg mix and then pat with the crumbs for a second time. Set aside and repeat with the remaining chicken.

Melt the butter and olive oil in a large non-stick frying pan over low-medium heat. Shallow-fry the chicken for 4-5 minutes each side or until golden and cooked through. Serve the chicken with lemon wedges and extra grated parmesan.

# GRILLED QUAIL WITH ROAST PUMPKIN SALAD

**SERVES 4**

*If you can't get hold of big, meaty jumbo quail, cook two smaller quail per person.*

1 kg (2 lb 4 oz) butternut pumpkin (squash), peeled, seeded
4 tbsp olive oil, plus extra to serve
4 x 200 g (7 oz) jumbo quail
3 spring onions (scallions), pale part only, finely sliced
1 red capsicum (pepper), seeded, very finely chopped
½ bunch coriander (cilantro), leaves picked
½ tsp chilli flakes
2 tbsp aged balsamic vinegar (8 years or older)

Heat the oven to 220°C (425°F). Cut the pumpkin into 2 cm (¾ in) cubes, drizzle with 2 tablespoons of the olive oil, season well and bake for 20 minutes or until tender and golden. Set aside to cool.

Heat the barbecue or a ridged cast-iron chargrill pan.

Place the quail breast-side down on a board. Use poultry shears or kitchen scissors to cut down either side of the backbone and discard. Turn the quail breast-side up and push down on the breastbone to flatten, then tuck in the wings. Repeat with the remaining quail, then season and rub with 1 tablespoon of the olive oil.

Grill the quail, breast-side down first, for 4–5 minutes on each side or until cooked through. Set aside and rest for 5 minutes.

In a bowl, toss the pumpkin with the spring onion, capsicum, coriander, chilli, balsamic vinegar and the remaining olive oil. Serve with the quail.

*'When you're cooking at home, the quality of your eating is all to do with the quality of your shopping.'*

# CRUMBED VEAL CUTLETS WITH PEPERONATA

**SERVES 4**

*During the Renaissance, Italians believed that gold was good for the heart, so the rich served their food covered with gold leaf. The poor did the next best thing - coated their cotoletta alla Milanese in breadcrumbs and fried it until crisp and golden. Serve this with a piquant peperonata and a side of roast pumpkin with lemon yoghurt (see page 171).*

175 g (6 oz) parmesan, finely grated
250 g (9 oz) fresh white breadcrumbs
3 eggs
125 ml (4 fl oz/$1/2$ cup) milk
100 g ($3^1/2$ oz) plain (all-purpose) flour, seasoned
4 x 200 g (7 oz) veal cutlets
150 g ($5^1/2$ oz) butter, preferably clarified
lemon cheeks, to serve

## PEPERONATA

6 red capsicums (peppers), roasted, peeled, juices reserved
4 tbsp olive oil
4 garlic cloves, sliced
2 onions, finely sliced
pinch of chilli flakes
150 ml (5 fl oz) tomato passata
2 tbsp aged red wine vinegar
60 g ($2^1/4$ oz) flaked almonds, roasted (optional)

Heat the oven to 180°C (350°F). To make the peperonata, coat the capsicums in 1 tablespoon of the olive oil and bake for 20 minutes or until softened. Remove and cover with foil for 30 minutes to steam. When cool, peel off and discard the skin, and strain the juices, discarding the seeds. Cut the flesh into strips. You can do this ahead of time, and store the capsicum strips in the fridge for up to 2 days.

Heat the remaining olive oil in a frying pan over medium heat, add the garlic, onion and chilli and cook for 10 minutes or until soft. Add the passata, the capsicum strips and their juices and cook for 15 minutes or until reduced. Remove from the heat, stir in the vinegar and scatter with the flaked almonds (if using).

To cook the veal, combine the parmesan and breadcrumbs in a bowl. In a separate bowl, whisk together the eggs and milk. Place the flour in a third bowl. Lightly flatten the veal with a meat mallet - do not make it too thin.

Season the veal, then dust with the flour. Dip in the egg, then coat with the breadcrumbs. Repeat the egg and the breadcrumb coatings. Heat the butter in a non-stick frying pan over low-medium heat and fry the veal for 8 minutes on each side or until golden and cooked.

Drain on paper towel, transfer to a baking tray and rest the veal in a warm place for 10 minutes. Serve with the peperonata and lemon cheeks.

# SNAPPER WITH FENNEL & ROMAN BEANS

**SERVES 4**

*Any firm, white-fleshed fish will get a lift from the fresh aniseed flavour of the fennel. Roman beans are also known as romano beans - they're flatter and longer than normal green beans, with an intense sweet green-bean flavour. Potatoes with garlic and parsley (see page 171) on the side are the perfect accompaniment.*

4 x 180 g (6½ oz) snapper fillets, boned, skin on
2½ tbsp olive oil, plus extra to serve
4 roman beans
250 g (9 oz) cherry tomatoes
12 basil leaves

**FENNEL PUREE**
2 tbsp olive oil
2 shallots, roughly chopped
1 garlic clove, finely sliced
1 fennel bulb, trimmed, finely sliced
100 ml (3½ fl oz) thin (pouring) cream

To make the fennel puree, heat the olive oil in a saucepan over medium heat. Add the shallots and garlic with a pinch of sea salt and cook for 5 minutes or until soft. Add the fennel and cook for a further 5 minutes. Add the cream and simmer until the fennel is soft. Process in a food processor or blender until smooth, and check seasoning.

Meanwhile, heat the oven to 200°C (400°F). Season the fish with sea salt and freshly ground black pepper.

Heat an ovenproof frying pan over high heat until smoking. Add the olive oil and cook the fish skin-side down for 1 minute, then transfer the pan to the oven. Cook for 4-6 minutes or until just cooked through.

Cut the roman beans on a diagonal into 1 cm (½ in) slices. Cook in boiling, salted water for 2-3 minutes or until tender. Drain and refresh in iced water and drain again.

Cut the cherry tomatoes in half and toss in a small bowl with the roman beans, basil, sea salt, freshly ground black pepper and a drizzle of olive oil.

Place the fennel puree on dinner plates, and arrange the fish and tomato salad on top.

# SARDINE BRUSCHETTA WITH PESTO

**SERVES 4**

*Bruschetta - charcoal-grilled bread rubbed with garlic and dressed with olive oil - is good enough on its own, or just with lightly stewed tomatoes. But add a few rich, oily sardines and a whack of pesto and it's the business.*

100 ml (3½ fl oz) extra virgin olive oil
3 garlic cloves, finely sliced
500 g (1 lb 2 oz) cherry tomatoes, cut in half
4 ciabatta slices
12 fresh sardine fillets
4 tbsp pesto (Basics, 255)

In a saucepan, heat 2 tablespoons of the olive oil, add the garlic and cook for 5 minutes or until fragrant. Add the tomatoes and 1 teaspoon of sea salt and cook for 10 minutes or until the tomatoes have broken down. Check seasoning, and keep warm.

Heat a barbecue or a cast-iron chargrill pan. Rub the ciabatta with 1 tablespoon of the olive oil, and grill on both sides until charred.

Rub the sardines with 1 tablespoon of the olive oil and lightly season with sea salt and freshly ground black pepper. Grill for 2 minutes on the skin side, then turn and cook for another 1 minute or until just cooked through.

Spoon the tomatoes over the grilled ciabatta, place the sardine fillets on top, spoon on the pesto and drizzle with the remaining olive oil.

# SALTIMBOCCA WITH SPINACH & LEMON

**SERVES 4**

*Saltimbocca means 'jump in the mouth' and that's exactly what these veal escalopes, lined with prosciutto and sage and drowned in lemony, buttery juices, will do. A lot of people throw capers at this dish as well; that's up to you and your caper threshold.*

8 long, thin slices prosciutto
8 x 100 g (3½ oz) escalopes of veal
8 sage leaves
2 tbsp olive oil
100 g (3½ oz) unsalted butter
200 g (7 oz) baby English spinach leaves
juice of ½ lemon

Place a slice of prosciutto flat on the bench, place a piece of veal across the middle and a sage leaf on top of the veal. Wrap the prosciutto around. Repeat with the remaining pieces.

Heat the olive oil in a frying pan over medium heat. Cook the veal for 3 minutes each side until just cooked, then rest in a warm place.

Meanwhile, melt 1 tablespoon of the butter in a small frying pan and cook the spinach for 2 minutes or until wilted.

Place the frying pan used to cook the veal back on the stove over medium heat and add the remaining butter. Heat until foaming, then squeeze in the lemon juice, stirring with a wooden spoon.

Cut each piece of veal in half diagonally and arrange next to the spinach. Spoon over the buttery pan juices and serve.

# CHICKEN & PROSCIUTTO ROTOLO WITH CHICORY

## SERVES 4

*This is great cold the next day, smashed into a bread roll for lunch.*

4 x 200 g (7 oz) skin-on chicken breast fillets
8 thin slices prosciutto
4 tbsp olive oil
1 bunch chicory or other bitter greens, roughly chopped
4 tbsp mascarpone
juice of 1/2 lemon

Heat the oven to 220°C (425°F).

Place each chicken breast between two pieces of plastic wrap and gently pound with the flat side of a meat mallet or rolling pin until about 2 mm (1/16 in) thick. Lay the prosciutto on the chicken and roll up, keeping the prosciutto on the inside of the chicken. Use toothpicks or skewers to hold the chicken in place. Repeat with the remaining chicken.

In an ovenproof frying pan, heat half the olive oil over medium heat. Lightly colour the chicken all over, then transfer the whole pan to the oven. Cook for 7 minutes, turning halfway through, or until the chicken is just cooked. Remove and allow the chicken to rest in the pan for 5 minutes.

Heat the remaining olive oil in a second frying pan over medium heat, add the chicory and season with sea salt and freshly ground black pepper. Cook for 2-3 minutes or until wilted.

To serve, transfer the chicken to a chopping board and return the pan to low heat. Add the mascarpone and warm gently, being careful not to boil. Remove any toothpicks or skewers and cut the chicken on the diagonal. Arrange on top of the chicory on dinner plates. Squeeze the lemon juice into the mascarpone and spoon over or around the chicory.

# MACKEREL WITH RADICCHIO & ORANGE

## SERVES 4

*Oily fish such as mackerel and sardines used to be regarded as second-rate. Now we know both how good they can taste, and how good they are for us.*

2 oranges
1 head of radicchio
2 red witlof (Belgian endive)
1 bunch watercress
100 ml (3 1/2 fl oz) extra virgin olive oil, plus extra to serve
8 fresh mackerel fillets

Squeeze the juice from 1 orange. Segment the second orange, starting by cutting off the skin and white pith with a sharp knife. Hold the fruit in the palm of your hand over a bowl, and make small, sharp, v-shaped cuts between each membrane, allowing the segments to slip out into the bowl. Discard the membrane.

Wash the radicchio and tear the leaves into bite-sized pieces. Remove the leaves from the witlof and cut into bite-sized pieces. Wash the watercress and tear into bite-sized sections.

Heat a heavy-based frying pan until it starts to smoke, then add the olive oil.

Season the mackerel fillets with sea salt and freshly ground black pepper and place in the pan skin-side down, reducing the heat to medium. Cook for about 2 minutes, then turn and cook for a further 2 minutes or until cooked.

Combine the radicchio, witlof, watercress and orange segments in a bowl and season with salt and pepper. Dress with the reserved orange juice and enough extra virgin olive oil to coat the leaves. Arrange the salad and mackerel on dinner plates and serve.

# OSSO BUCO
# IN BIANCO
## SERVES 4

*The common view of Italian cooking is that
everything comes in one ubiquitous, all-conquering
'red sauce', or sauce napoletana. That's more true of
the tomato-rich south, but in the north, most dishes
are cooked 'in bianco' - in white, without tomatoes.
This rich stew pairs well with grilled mushrooms
with parsley (see page 171).*

100 g (3¹/2 oz) butter, chopped
3 onions, finely chopped
6 garlic cloves, finely sliced
4 anchovies in oil, drained
4 celery stalks, finely chopped
¹/2 tsp chilli flakes
100 g (3¹/2 oz) pancetta, finely chopped
50 g (1³/4 oz) piece parmesan rind,
   or 20 g (³/4 oz) parmesan, grated
750 ml (26 fl oz/3 cups) dry white wine
1.25 litres (44 fl oz/5 cups) veal or chicken stock
8 x 150 g (5¹/2 oz) pieces osso buco
80 g (2³/4 oz) plain (all-purpose) flour, seasoned
2¹/2 tbsp olive oil, plus extra to serve
400 g (14 oz) baby potatoes
2 tbsp gremolata (Basics, 255)

Heat the butter in a flameproof casserole over
medium heat and cook the onion, garlic and anchovies
for 5 minutes or until soft. Add the celery, chilli and
1 tablespoon of sea salt and cook for a further 5 minutes
or until the celery is soft. Add the pancetta, parmesan
and wine and reduce by two-thirds. Add the stock and
bring to the boil.

Heat the oven to 150°C (300°F). Dust the osso buco
in flour and shake off the excess. Heat the olive oil in
a large frying pan over medium-high heat, and brown
the osso buco on both sides. Add the osso buco to the
liquid, cover with a lid or seal with foil and cook in the
oven for 3 hours or until the meat starts to come away
from the bone.

Place the potatoes in a large saucepan of boiling, salted
water and bring to the boil. Simmer for 20 minutes or
until tender. Cut into quarters.

When the osso buco is cooked, pick out the bone
(and the parmesan rind if used) and discard. Combine
with the potatoes, drizzle with olive oil and serve with
the gremolata.

# CRISP-SKIN SALMON WITH BEANS

**SERVES 4**

*The mix of beans in this dish is a good foil for the rich oiliness of fresh salmon or ocean trout.*

100 g (3½ oz) dried borlotti (cranberry) beans
100 g (3½ oz) dried kidney beans
200 g (7 oz) dried cannellini beans
1 onion, peeled, quartered
1 carrot, cut into 2 cm (¾ in) pieces
2 celery stalks, cut into 2 cm (¾ in) pieces
10 garlic cloves, peeled
1 bunch thyme
olive oil
4 x 200 g (7 oz) salmon fillets, pin-boned
2 tbsp butter
juice of ½ lemon
1 bunch flat-leaf parsley, finely chopped

Combine the beans and cover in twice their volume in water. Leave to soak overnight, then drain.

Fill a large saucepan with 3 litres (105 fl oz/12 cups) of cold water. Add the beans, onion, carrot, celery, garlic and thyme. Bring to the boil over medium heat, then simmer for 2½ hours or until tender. Drain and cool, discarding any larger vegetables or herbs.

Heat a heavy-based frying pan over high heat. When the pan is smoking, add just enough oil to coat the bottom of the pan. Season the salmon fillets with sea salt and freshly ground black pepper and place in the pan skin-side down, pressing it down so the skin stays flat.

When the salmon is about two-thirds cooked, reduce the heat to medium, turn over and cook for a further minute, leaving the inside a little pink.

Meanwhile, heat the beans, butter, salt and pepper over medium heat for 5 minutes or until hot. Add the lemon juice and parsley, and divide between plates.

Arrange the salmon, skin-side up, on top, drizzle with olive oil and serve.

# PESCE AL FORNO WITH OLIVES & POTATOES

**SERVES 4**

*We always have whole fish on the menu if we can. It's important that people don't get scared of them, and continue to appreciate the fact that everything tastes better when cooked on the bone.*

800 g (1 lb 12 oz) baby potatoes
4 plate-sized whole fish (eg baby snapper)
4 tbsp salsa verde (Basics, 256)
2 tbsp kalamata olives
1 lemon, cut into wedges
extra virgin olive oil, to serve

Heat the oven to 200°C (400°F). Cook the potatoes in boiling, salted water for 15 minutes or until tender. Drain, cool slightly, then cut in half.

Use a sharp knife to trim the fins off the fish and make several short, shallow slashes through the skin on each side. Rub the fish with 1 teaspoon of sea salt and the salsa verde.

Place the fish in a roasting tin with the potatoes and bake for 10-15 minutes or until nearly cooked, turning the fish after the first 5 minutes.

Add the olives and cook for a further 3 minutes or until the flesh of the fish breaks away easily from the bone with a fork.

Transfer the fish and potatoes to dinner plates, scatter with the olives and lemon wedges, drizzle with extra virgin olive oil, and serve.

# LAMB SHANKS WITH CARROT & SWEDE

**SERVES 4**

*Lamb shanks sound more Aussie than Italian, but Italian sheep have shanks, too, called stinchi di agnello. Make a mental note of this mash - it's very good with many things other than shanks, Italian or otherwise.*

4 lamb shanks, trimmed of excess fat
50 g (1³/₄ oz) plain (all-purpose) flour
1 tbsp olive oil
2 garlic cloves, finely sliced
700 ml (24 fl oz) tomato passata
4 good sprigs rosemary, leaves picked
250 ml (9 fl oz/1 cup) beef or chicken stock or water
500 g (1 lb 2 oz) carrots
500 g (1 lb 2 oz) swede (rutabaga)
2 tbsp butter

Heat the oven to 180°C (350°F). Dust the shanks with the flour then shake off any excess.

Heat the olive oil in a casserole or ovenproof saucepan and brown the shanks over medium heat, turning occasionally, for 8 minutes or until browned all over.

Add the garlic, passata, rosemary, a good pinch of sea salt and stock to just cover the shanks, then seal with a lid or foil.

Cook for 3 hours, turning halfway, or until the meat is tender and comes away from the bone.

Roughly chop the carrots and the swede.

To make the mash, cook the carrot and swede in simmering, salted water for 20 minutes or until tender. Drain, then return to the pan off the heat. Add the butter, season with sea salt and freshly ground black pepper and roughly mash. Serve the shanks on the mash with plenty of the tomato sauce.

# PAN-FRIED SKATE WITH PINE MUSHROOMS

**SERVES 4**

*Because pine mushrooms are only around in autumn, feel free to use other mushrooms such as king mushrooms, swiss browns or even fresh shiitake mushrooms instead.*

1 lemon
4 tbsp olive oil
4 x 280 g (10 oz) pieces of skate, on the bone
200 g (7 oz) pine mushrooms, sliced
2 tbsp unsalted butter
8 anchovies in oil, drained
2 tbsp gremolata (Basics, 255)
2 tbsp salted baby capers, rinsed

To segment the lemon, cut off the skin and white pith with a sharp knife. Hold the fruit in the palm of your hand over a bowl, and make small, sharp, v-shaped cuts between each membrane, allowing the segments to slip out into the bowl. Discard the membrane.

Heat half the olive oil in a heavy-based frying pan. Season the fish and cook for 5-8 minutes on each side, depending on thickness, or until just cooked through. Remove from the pan and allow to rest.

Wipe the pan clean, add the remaining olive oil and cook the sliced mushrooms for 3 minutes or until nearly cooked. Add the butter and anchovies and cook for 1 minute, then add the gremolata, capers and lemon segments, tossing well to combine.

Spoon the mushrooms and sauce over the fish and serve.

# SMOKED TROUT FISH CAKES WITH SOFT-BOILED EGG

**SERVES 4 AS A MAIN OR 8 AS A STARTER**

*Fish cakes are like burgers - everyone loves them; old and young, male and female. These make a good lunch, dinner, supper or weekend brunch.*

600 g (1 lb 5 oz) all-purpose potatoes (eg desiree), peeled, quartered

500 g (1 lb 2 oz) whole smoked rainbow trout, skin and bones removed, flesh flaked

1 bunch flat-leaf parsley, finely chopped

100 g (3½ oz) aioli (Basics, 252)

½ red (Spanish) onion, finely chopped

1 tbsp salted baby capers, rinsed

½ bunch tarragon, leaves finely chopped

½ bunch chives, finely chopped

juice of ½ lemon

8 eggs

150 g (5½ oz) plain (all-purpose) flour

200 g (7 oz) fresh white breadcrumbs

vegetable oil, for shallow-frying

½ bunch watercress, sprigs picked

Cook the potatoes in boiling, salted water until tender. Drain, then mash in a bowl.

Flake the smoked trout flesh apart with your fingers, then combine with the potato and half the parsley. Season well, shape into eight 8 cm (3¼ in) wide patties and refrigerate for 3 hours.

To make the herb aioli, combine the aioli, onion, capers, herbs and lemon juice in a bowl, season well and refrigerate.

Lightly whisk four of the eggs in a shallow bowl. Place the flour and breadcrumbs in separate shallow bowls. Gently dust the fish cakes with the flour, dip them into the whisked egg, then finally coat in breadcrumbs.

Cook the remaining eggs in a saucepan of boiling water for 5½ minutes then drain and refresh in iced water. Peel under running water when cool enough to handle.

Fill a frying pan with vegetable oil to a level of 3 cm (1¼ in), and heat to 180°C (350°F). Cook the fish cakes, in batches, for 2 minutes on each side or until golden. Drain on paper towel.

To serve, cut the soft-boiled eggs in half. Serve the fish cakes with the soft-boiled eggs, watercress and herb aioli.

# SEARED TUNA WITH ZUCCHINI & BASIL

**SERVES 4**

*Zucchini flowers, cherry tomatoes, basil... it must be summer. It's a toss-up whether cherry tomatoes are best raw and eaten in the hand as you're passing through the kitchen, or gently cooked into a buttery tomato sauce to go with tuna.*

3 tbsp butter, chopped
5 garlic cloves, finely sliced
400 g (14 oz) cherry tomatoes, halved
100 ml (3¹/₂ fl oz) tomato passata
8 female zucchini (courgette) flowers, with zucchini attached
4 x 160 g (5³/₄ oz) thick-cut tuna steaks, skinned
3 tbsp olive oil
2 tbsp green olives, pitted, chopped
8 basil leaves

Heat the butter in a frying pan over medium heat, add the garlic and cook for 1-2 minutes or until soft and fragrant but not coloured. Add the cherry tomatoes and cook for 10 minutes or until softened. Add the passata, bring to a simmer, then remove from the heat and season.

Separate and reserve the flowers from the zucchini, then finely slice the zucchini lengthwise. Cook in boiling, salted water for 1 minute, drain, refresh in iced water, drain again and set aside.

Heat a frying pan until smoking and season the tuna. Add 2 tablespoons of the olive oil to the hot pan, add the tuna and cook for 2 minutes each side for rare, or until cooked to your liking.

Place the zucchini and olives in a bowl, tear the flowers and basil on top, season and toss with the remaining olive oil. To serve, divide the warm tomato sauce among dinner plates and top with the zucchini salad and the tuna.

# CONTORNI

One day some brilliant person will open a restaurant that specialises in contorni, those simple dishes that are meant to go 'on the side' of the main dish. Because how many times have you enjoyed the side dish more than the main dish? There is something so satisfying about taking a vegetable in season, cooking it simply and serving it generously in the middle of the table for all to share. I've seen people in our restaurants order three or four contorni and a pasta or polenta dish and treat them all the same, eating a little bit of this and a little bit of that, with not too much of any one thing.

In Italy, there is sometimes little difference between the antipasti and the contorni, and you can make a very fine meal by covering the table with a few antipasti dishes and some grilled mushrooms, wilted radicchio and roast pumpkin.

What you choose depends on the season, of course, but if you are cooking one of these dishes to go on the side of a simple main course, go for a contrasting flavour or texture. A crumbed veal cutlet, for instance, would be best matched by a crisp, tangy coleslaw; while a rich, slow-braised stew would get a lift from something as simple as green beans with toasted almonds, or steamed broccolini with anchovy crumbs. Grilled mushrooms with parsley are great with anything off the barbecue, and grilled, marinated vegetables add an almost fruity, earthy complexity to a simple fish or lamb dish. Potatoes go with everything, especially when they're crisp, crunchy, golden and tossed with garlic and parsley. Oh yeah.

## CAFÉ SOPRA COLESLAW
### SERVES 4 AS SIDE DISH, PICTURED PAGE 147

Toss 200 g (7 oz) finely shaved savoy cabbage and 100 g (3½ oz) finely shaved red cabbage with ½ finely sliced red (Spanish) onion, 2 grated carrots, 2 tbsp roughly chopped flat-leaf parsley, sea salt, freshly ground black pepper and 150 g (5½ oz) aioli (Basics, 252) until well coated. Lighten with a dash of water if need be, and serve.

## GREEN BEANS WITH TOASTED ALMONDS
### SERVES 4 AS SIDE DISH, PICTURED PAGE 167

Cook 250 g (9 oz) trimmed green beans in simmering, salted water for 2-3 minutes or until tender but still with a little bite. Drain well and toss with 1 tbsp lemon vinaigrette (Basics, 254), sea salt and freshly ground black pepper. Toast 2 tbsp almonds in a dry frying pan until golden, and scatter on top.

## GRILLED MARINATED VEGETABLES
### SERVES 4 AS SIDE DISH, PICTURED PAGE 138

Heat a barbecue or chargrill pan until hot. Finely shave 1 zucchini (courgette) lengthways. Deseed 1 red capsicum (pepper) and cut into four. Slice 1 eggplant (aubergine) crossways, and cut half a red (Spanish) onion into six wedges. Drizzle the cut vegetables with 2 tbsp extra virgin olive oil and cook on the hot grill in batches until tender. Transfer to a bowl and add the zest of 1 lemon, 1 crushed garlic clove, 8 mint leaves, a pinch of chilli flakes, sea salt, black pepper and another drizzle of extra virgin olive oil. Serve hot or at room temperature.

## GRILLED MUSHROOMS
## WITH PARSLEY
SERVES 4 AS SIDE DISH, PICTURED PAGE 159

Heat a barbecue or chargrill pan until hot. Drizzle
4 large flat mushrooms with 2 tbsp extra virgin olive oil
and season with sea salt and freshly ground black pepper.
Grill for 3 minutes on each side or until tender. Scatter
with 2 tbsp roughly chopped flat-leaf parsley and serve.

## POTATOES WITH GARLIC
## & PARSLEY
SERVES 4 AS SIDE DISH, PICTURED PAGE 152

Cook 100 g (3½ oz) baby potatoes (skin on) in simmering,
salted water for 15 minutes or until tender, then drain
and cool. Heat a deep-fryer or a saucepan of vegetable oil
to 180°C (350°F). Cut the potatoes into quarters and fry
until golden. Drain on paper towel, then toss in a bowl
with 1 crushed garlic clove, 2 tbsp finely chopped flat-leaf
parsley and sea salt. Serve hot.

## RADICCHIO
## WITH AGED BALSAMIC
SERVES 4 AS SIDE DISH, PICTURED PAGE 129

In a bowl, whisk together 3 tbsp extra virgin olive oil,
1 tbsp aged balsamic vinegar (8 years or older), sea salt
and freshly ground pepper. Discard the green leaves of
1 head of radicchio, and wash and dry the red leaves.
Toss in the vinaigrette and serve. Radicchio is also good
cut lengthways into quarters, coated with olive oil and
charred on a barbecue. Serve with fish, chicken, pork,
pasta and polenta, or simply with a slice of prosciutto
or oven-crisped pancetta on top.

## ROAST PUMPKIN
## WITH LEMON YOGHURT
SERVES 4 AS SIDE DISH, PICTURED PAGE 150

Heat the oven to 220°C (425°F). Cut 1 kg (2 lb 4 oz)
peeled and seeded butternut pumpkin (squash)
into 2 cm (¾ in) cubes, drizzle with 2 tbsp extra
virgin olive oil, and toss with sea salt and freshly
ground black pepper. Bake for 15 minutes or until
golden and tender.

Stir 1 crushed garlic clove into 100 g (3½ oz) plain
yoghurt, arrange the pumpkin on top, scatter with
1 tbsp finely chopped flat-leaf parsley and drizzle with
2 tbsp lemon vinaigrette (Basics, 254). Serve with roast
chicken, fish, lamb, or on the side of a simple meal
of pizza or homemade pasta.

## STEAMED BROCCOLINI
## WITH ANCHOVY CRUMBS
SERVES 4 AS SIDE DISH, PICTURED PAGE 130

Heat 3 tbsp extra virgin olive oil in a frying pan and
add 4 drained anchovies in oil. Cook over low heat for
2 minutes or until melted, add 1 finely chopped garlic
clove and cook for a further minute. Add ½ cup (30 g/
1 oz) fresh breadcrumbs and fry, stirring, until golden
brown - you may need to use a little more olive oil.

Cook 2 bunches trimmed broccolini in boiling, salted
water for 2-3 minutes or until tender. Season with sea
salt and freshly ground black pepper. Scatter the anchovy
crumbs over the broccolini and serve.

Two tips: one, this is fantastic with a fried egg on top;
and two, swap the broccolini for fresh asparagus
when in season.

# PIZZA

PIZZA ALLA M...

ROSEMARY & GARLIC Fo...

PROSCIUTTO &...

# PIZZA BASE

**MAKES 4**

*Some Italians like their pizza swimming in olive oil; we don't. We like our pizza to be thin, crisp and easy to digest. It's all about the crusty raised edges - what Italians call the cornicione.*

*To get that result, pizza has to cook fast, so you have to crank up your oven as high as it can go. You can't achieve the fierce heat (about 500°C/930°F) of a commercial pizza oven, but you can get closer to it by using a pizza stone or an untreated, unsealed terracotta tile that you can preheat, which will deliver a more concentrated heat than a metal baking tray. You can also cook the base for a few minutes first to 'set' it, then top it with the final ingredients and finish the cooking.*

*Our pizza chefs use fresh yeast for the pizza base, which gives a wonderfully light dough that feels almost alive. If you can't find fresh yeast (specialist bakers' shops will have it) then use dried yeast instead, which can be kept to hand.*

*And don't be scared to get in there and work the dough with your hands - pizza dough needs a lot of love.*

*You'll want a great tomato sauce for the top - ours changes depending on the season, but is usually a combination of fresh tomatoes, canned tomatoes and tomato sugo. Yes, you can use tomato paste or puree, but it's usually quite acidic - better to cook up a pot of your own sugo and freeze it in batches for your next pizza party. You don't need a lot of herbs, just a couple of torn basil leaves or a pinch of oregano.*

*The only other thing to remember is to not overload your pizza - it is rarely improved after the first three main ingredients are added.*

**2 g ($^{1}/_{16}$ oz) fresh yeast or 7 g ($^{3}/_{16}$ oz) dried yeast**
**650 g (1 lb 7 oz) '00' flour, plus extra for dusting**
**3 tbsp extra virgin olive oil**

Mix the fresh yeast and 400 ml (14 fl oz) of lukewarm water in a bowl until dissolved.

In a second bowl, mix the flour and 2 teaspoons of salt and make a well in the centre.

Slowly add the yeast mixture to the flour, drawing in the flour with your fingers until the dough forms into a mass.

(If using dried yeast, mix the flour, dried yeast and 2 teaspoons of salt in a bowl, and make a well in the centre. Slowly add 400 ml (14 fl oz) of water to the well, drawing in the dry ingredients with your fingers until the dough forms into a mass.)

Add the olive oil and continue to mix until all the oil is absorbed.

Turn out onto a floured work surface, and knead the dough with your hands, pushing the dough away with the heel of your hand as you pull the rest closer to you, turning the dough a quarter turn each time, until it is soft, smooth and resilient and no longer sticky, about 10 minutes.

Transfer the dough to a clean bowl, cover with a clean, damp tea towel (dish towel) and leave for 3 hours at room temperature.

Cut the dough into 4 x 250 g (9 oz) pieces and roll into balls. Place the balls on a tray, wrap the tray with plastic wrap and leave for 2 hours, to double in size. Any unused balls of pizza dough can be covered in plastic wrap and stored in the fridge for up to 24 hours.

Place the pizza stone (if using) in the oven to pre-heat, and heat the oven to its highest setting.

On a floured bench, roll out your dough with a rolling pin to a 5 mm (¼ in) thick circle.

Now add the toppings and transfer to the pizza stone or a baking tray. Bake for 10-12 minutes or until the base is crisp. Cut into wedges and serve.

# PIZZA WITH CHORIZO, SALAMI & HAM

**MAKES 1 PIZZA**

*I love how everyone's hands just reach out automatically as soon as a pizza hits the centre of the table. This pizza is a beautiful and somewhat spicy combination of meats, but really, you can use whatever Italian salumi you have to hand.*

250 g (9 oz) oven-ready pizza dough (page 175)
100 g (3¹/₂ oz) salsa di pomodoro (Basics, 256)
8 thin slices salami
50 g (1³/₄ oz) smoked ham, shredded
100 g (3¹/₂ oz) buffalo mozzarella, drained, sliced
1 semi-dried chorizo sausage, sliced

Place the pizza stone (if using) in the oven to pre-heat, and heat the oven to its highest setting.

On a floured bench, roll out your dough with a rolling pin to a 5 mm (¼ in) thick circle. Transfer to the pizza stone or a baking tray.

Use the back of a spoon to spread the salsa di pomodoro over the top, leaving a little border free around the edges.

Arrange the salami, ham and mozzarella on the base and top with the chorizo. Transfer to the pizza stone or a baking tray and bake for 10 minutes or until the base is crisp, and serve.

*'The thing about pizza is that it gets people together. Everyone gathers around; it's very sociable.'*

# PIZZA ALLA MARINARA

**MAKES 1 PIZZA**

*Not seafood, as the name might suggest, but basic tomato, garlic, oil and oregano, done in the simple style of the old-time sailors. We add anchovy and basil as a humble improvement on the original.*

250 g (9 oz) oven-ready pizza dough (page 175)
100 g (3<sup>1</sup>/2 oz) salsa di pomodoro (Basics, 256)
6 anchovies in oil, drained,
  cut in half lengthways
1 garlic clove, finely sliced
1 tsp dried oregano
6 basil leaves
extra virgin olive oil, to serve

Place the pizza stone (if using) in the oven to pre-heat, and heat the oven to its highest setting.

On a floured bench, roll out your dough with a rolling pin to a 5 mm (¼ in) thick circle.

Use the back of a spoon to spread the salsa di pomodoro over the top, leaving a little border free around the edges. Arrange the anchovies and garlic on top. Transfer to the pizza stone or a baking tray and bake for 10 minutes or until the base is crisp. Scatter with the oregano and basil, drizzle with extra virgin olive oil and serve.

# PIZZA WITH PROSCIUTTO & ROCKET

**MAKES 1 PIZZA**

*Italians would never add prosciutto to a pizza before it goes into the oven, because it gets too crisp and salty. So they came up with this idea: draping it over the super-hot pizza as soon as it leaves the oven, so that the heat just permeates the prosciutto without killing it.*

250 g (9 oz) oven-ready pizza dough (page 175)
100 g (3<sup>1</sup>/2 oz) salsa di pomodoro (Basics, 256)
85 g (3 oz) buffalo mozzarella, drained, sliced
6 thin slices prosciutto
handful rocket (arugula)
handful parmesan shavings
extra virgin olive oil, to serve

Place the pizza stone (if using) in the oven to pre-heat, and heat the oven to its highest setting.

On a floured bench, roll out your dough with a rolling pin to a 5 mm (¼ in) thick circle.

Use the back of a spoon to spread the salsa di pomodoro over the top, leaving a little border free around the edges. Arrange the mozzarella on top. Transfer to the pizza stone or a baking tray and bake for 10 minutes or until the base is crisp. Immediately layer the prosciutto on top, scatter with the rocket and parmesan, add a drizzle of extra virgin olive oil and serve.

# ROSEMARY & GARLIC FOCACCIA

## MAKES 1 FOCACCIA

*This light, golden bread seems to go so well with everything else Italian, especially with the simple topping of garlic and rosemary traditional to Liguria.*

**250 g (9 oz) oven-ready pizza dough (page 175)**
**2 tbsp extra virgin olive oil**
**1 garlic clove, finely sliced**
**1 tbsp rosemary leaves**

Place the dough on a lightly oiled baking tray. Stretch it out into a circle or rectangle, about 1 cm (½ in) thick. Cover with a clean tea towel (dish towel) and leave to rise for about 45 minutes.

Heat the oven to 230°C (450°F). Use the tips of your fingers to prod the dough, making rows of small indentations about 1 cm (½ in) apart. Brush generously with the olive oil and scatter with the garlic, rosemary and some sea salt. Bake for 8-10 minutes or until crisp and golden on top. Use a pizza cutter to cut into strips or wedges, and eat warm or at room temperature.

# PIZZA BIANCA WITH FRESH FIG & PROSCIUTTO

## MAKES 1 PIZZA

*A pizza without tomato sauce is called a white pizza, or pizza bianca. It's ideal for lighter, fresher toppings such as this summertime favourite: the sweetness of the figs matched by the savouriness of prosciutto.*

**250 g (9 oz) oven-ready pizza dough (page 175)**
**100 g (3½ oz) buffalo mozzarella, drained, sliced**
**2 figs**
**6 thin slices prosciutto**
**aged balsamic vinegar (8 years or older), to serve**

Place the pizza stone (if using) in the oven to pre-heat, and heat the oven to its highest setting.

On a floured bench, roll out your dough with a rolling pin to a 5 mm (¼ in) thick circle.

Arrange the mozzarella on top. Transfer to the pizza stone or a baking tray and bake for 10 minutes or until the base is crisp. Cut the figs into six wedges each, or tear into bite-sized pieces.

Arrange the prosciutto and figs on top, drizzle with balsamic vinegar and serve immediately.

# PIZZA MARGHERITA

**MAKES 1 PIZZA**

*It's the most classic pizza there is, topped with tomato, mozzarella and basil. Designed for Queen Margherita of Savoy in 1889, it has never, ever, been bettered.*

**250 g (9 oz) oven-ready pizza dough (page 175)**
**100 g (3½ oz) salsa di pomodoro (Basics, 256)**
**100 g (3½ oz) buffalo mozzarella, drained, sliced**
**1 tbsp grated parmesan**
**6 basil leaves**
**1 tbsp extra virgin olive oil**

Place the pizza stone (if using) in the oven to pre-heat, and heat the oven to its highest setting.

On a floured bench, roll out your dough with a rolling pin to a 5 mm (¼ in) thick circle.

Use the back of a spoon to spread the salsa di pomodoro over the top, leaving a little border free around the edges. Arrange the mozzarella on top and scatter with the parmesan. Transfer to the pizza stone or a baking tray and bake for 10 minutes or until the crust is crisp. Scatter with the basil leaves, drizzle with the olive oil and serve.

*'Pizza made by hand, cooked at hell-fire heat and eaten on the spot is a world apart.'*

# FORMAGGI

If there had to be only one Italian cheese in the world, then it would have to be Parmigiano Reggiano, and it would need to be at least a couple of years old.

At about two years, a true parmesan begins to develop that unique umami character and extraordinary crystalline crunch that keeps you coming back for more. While Parmigiano Reggiano is the most noble of cheeses, I'm also fond of Grana Padano, its more affordable cousin. It's like the difference between a fine arabica coffee bean and a stronger, more obvious robusta bean - each has its own appeal. When we grate cheese for pasta at Café Sopra, we use the Grana, but when we put out a wedge of cheese with an aperitivo, it's Parmigiano Reggiano.

But really, all Italian cheeses are good. I love the savoury, semi-hard and hard cheeses, and mellow cheeses such as Piave, Montasio and Asiago. Each cheese is typical of the milk of its region, so that the cheeses you try as you travel through Italy will change from buffalo's milk to cow's milk, goat's milk and sheep's milk. Italians are so proud of their cheese, they will serve just one small piece of one particular local or regional cheese at the end of a meal. There's no big cheese trolley, no French brie and no huge fuss made; just the one cheese they recommend for that time of the year, to be eaten with a knife and fork, on its own. I prefer some crusty bread or some Misura crackers from Italy with my cheese, but I love that they make the cheese the hero.

Fresh fruit also works well with cheese, especially the ripe stone fruits of summer. The sweet acid of ripe peaches and nectarines cuts through the fat of cheese. Celery hearts go well, too, as do walnuts, but they have to be fresh, and they have to be cracked at the table, not beforehand. If you don't have a nut cracker, just pick up two walnuts in the palm of your hand and squeeze them against each other - one walnut will crack the other open.

These are some of the cheeses we love and always have in stock.

## ASIAGO
A semi-fat cow's milk cheese named after the area in the Veneto region where it is made. It can be a smooth and springy young cheese (Asiago Pressato) or hard, crumbly and matured (Asiago d'Allevo).

## BURRATA
Originally made with buffalo milk, burrata is a fresh Italian curd cheese similar to mozzarella, from the southern Italian region of Puglia. While still warm, the cheese is formed into a pouch and filled with fresh cream and soft rags of curd. When cut, the rich, milky liquid will ooze out onto the plate.

## GORGONZOLA
A distinctive blue-vein cow's milk cheese from Lombardy, gorgonzola is a beautifully crafted cheese. The piccante, which is matured for 90 days, needs to be handled with care, or all that blue can ruin your red. Gorgonzola dolce, which is matured for only 20 days, is softer and sweeter, and goes well with fresh pears. In southern Italy, they drizzle local honey over gorgonzola dolce as a stunning end to the meal.

## GRANA PADANO
Made throughout Italy's north, Grana Padano is similar to Parmigiano Reggiano, but is less complex and time-consuming to make, being aged for only about six months. It's most commonly used for cooking and for snacking on while waiting for the pasta water to boil.

## MONTASIO
A semi-soft cow's milk cheese from Friuli. An equally good version is produced in the Veneto region. The younger, softer Montasio is good for the table, while the harder, mature Montasio is good for the kitchen.

## MOZZARELLA DI BUFALA
The best mozzarella is produced in Campania from water buffalo milk, formed into round, squidgy balls of sweet, lush and juicy white curd. In Italy, they like to eat it the same day it is made. Cow's milk mozzarella, fior di latte, is good for cooking and melting.

## PARMIGIANO REGGIANO

The king of Italian cheeses was first produced in the area between Parma and Reggio Emilia in Italy's north. It is made today in the same way it has been for centuries, turned into large 30 kilogram wheels, which develop a lovely straw colour and a mellow, rich taste.

## PECORINO

Made from sheep's milk exclusively, with a salty flavour and crumbly texture, pecorino is produced throughout central and southern Italy. The best known are pecorino romano, pecorino sardo and pecorino Toscano. In the south, they'd rather grate pecorino than Parmigiano. You can't really compare the two; they're chalk and cheese.

## PIAVE

This nutty, straw-coloured cheese is named after the Piave river in the Veneto. Its flavour intensifies as the cheese ages, going through four distinct stages. At its oldest (and strongest) it is known as stravecchio.

## PROVOLONE

A supple cow's milk cheese produced originally in the Basilicata region, provolone is made in a wide variety of shapes and sizes. It may be aged for a few months or up to a year. The longer it is aged the yellower it is and the sharper the flavour.

## RICOTTA

A by-product of other Italian cheeses, ricotta is produced from the leftover whey and re-cooked. It can be made from goat's, sheep's or cow's milk and is used in both sweet and savoury dishes. It is pure white and creamy when fresh, but becomes hard and salty when aged.

## TALEGGIO

Produced in Lombardy from cow's milk, taleggio has a strong and unique fragrance with a creamy and salty texture and a distinctive reddish crust. Taleggio is a luscious, rich, full-bodied cheese, but you really have to be in the mood for it.

*'Italians are so proud of their cheese, they will serve just one small piece of one particular local or regional cheese at the end of a meal, to be eaten with a knife and fork, on its own.'*

# PIZZA WITH POTATO, SALSICCE & PECORINO

**MAKES 1 PIZZA**

*Whoever came up with the idea of adding finely sliced potato to a pizza should get a medal. It sounds unlikely, but it's just the most fabulous combination, especially with Italian pork sausage as well.*

250 g (9 oz) oven-ready pizza dough (page 175)
1 thick pork sausage, skinned
100 g (3½ oz) buffalo mozzarella, drained, sliced
2 small potatoes, boiled, cooled, sliced
1 tbsp shaved pecorino
extra virgin olive oil, to serve

Place the pizza stone (if using) in the oven to pre-heat, and heat the oven to its highest setting.

On a floured bench, roll out your dough with a rolling pin to a 5 mm (¼ in) thick circle.

Shape the skinned sausage meat into small, bite-sized meatballs. Cook the meatballs in the oven for 5 minutes, which should nearly cook them through.

Arrange the mozzarella, potato and meatballs on the pizza. Transfer to the pizza stone or a baking tray and bake for 10 minutes or until the base is crisp.

Top with the pecorino, drizzle with extra virgin olive oil and serve.

*'Pizza is people's food. You can't beat it.'*

# FOCACCIA WITH ZUCCHINI & MINT

**MAKES 1 FOCACCIA**

*Italians are funny about focaccia. Our pizza chefs never treat it as if it were pizza, and always slice it in an entirely different way so you can pick it up in bite-sized bits that are perfect with an aperitivo.*

2 zucchini (courgettes)
3 tbsp extra virgin olive oil
250 g (9 oz) oven-ready pizza dough (page 175)
1 garlic clove, finely grated
3 tbsp picked mint leaves

Roughly grate the zucchini, season with sea salt and freshly ground black pepper, then cover with the olive oil and set aside.

Place the pizza stone (if using) in the oven to pre-heat, and heat the oven to 230°C (450°F).

On a floured bench, roll out your dough with a rolling pin to a 5 mm (¼ in) thick circle.

Top the focaccia base with 1 tablespoon of the olive oil marinade, the garlic and a sprinkle of sea salt. Transfer to the pizza stone or baking tray and bake for 8-10 minutes or until crisp and golden on top. Scatter the zucchini and a little of the marinade on top, then top with the mint leaves and serve.

CELERY HEART, BABY COS &
ZUCCHINI FLOWER

# INSALATA
# e
# VERDURA

SHAVED FENNEL w WHITE

# BEETROOT, GREEN BEANS, LENTILS & ALMONDS

**SERVES 4**

*Love, love, love this salad. It's punchy, it's fresh, it has protein, and in line with the newly sensible thinking about eating, it uses meat more as a garnish than as the main event. It's also good without meat, of course.*

16 green beans, trimmed
8 thin slices pancetta
400 g (14 oz) braised lentils (Basics, 253)
1/4 bunch mint, leaves picked, roughly chopped
100 g (3 1/2 oz) watercress
60 g (2 1/4 oz) almonds, toasted
100 ml (3 1/2 fl oz) lemon vinaigrette (Basics, 254)

**PICKLED BEETROOT**
1 bunch beetroot (beets), washed, trimmed
300 ml (10 1/2 fl oz) red wine vinegar
300 ml (10 1/2 fl oz) red wine
2 tbsp brown sugar
2 bay leaves
2 garlic cloves
10 whole black peppercorns

To pickle the beetroot, place all the ingredients in a non-reactive saucepan with 300 ml (10 1/2 fl oz) of water and 1 teaspoon of sea salt and bring to the boil over medium heat. Reduce the heat and simmer for 45 minutes or until the beetroots are tender. Allow them to cool in the liquid, then drain, peel and cut into small wedges. You can store the beetroot in the liquid, in the fridge, for up to 1 week.

Cook the beans in simmering, salted water for 3 minutes or until tender, then drain and roughly chop.

Heat the oven to 180°C (350°F). Lay the pancetta between two ovenproof wire cake racks to keep it flat, and place on a baking tray. Bake for 6-8 minutes or until crisp.

To serve, spoon the lentils into a shallow bowl, place a mound of beetroot in the middle and top with the beans, mint, watercress, almonds and pancetta. Season and drizzle with a generous amount of the lemon vinaigrette.

# SHAVED BABY CABBAGE WITH AGED BALSAMIC VINEGAR

**SERVES 4**

*The local trend for shaved baby cabbage was started by an old mate of mine, John Wilson, years ago, and is now one of our biggest sellers. Because the cabbage is shaved so finely, it takes on the dressing beautifully. A heap of freshly grated parmesan in with it doesn't hurt, either.*

**2 x 250 g (9 oz) baby cabbages or 500 g (1 lb 2 oz) small savoy cabbage**
**100 g (3½ oz) parmesan, grated**
**100 ml (3½ fl oz) lemon vinaigrette (Basics, 254)**
**aged balsamic vinegar (8 years or older), to serve**

Discard the outer leaves of the cabbages, cut the remainder in quarters and core.

Use a mandolin or sharp knife to shave the cabbage as finely as possible.

Place the cabbage in a bowl with the parmesan and pour over the lemon vinaigrette. Season, then toss well to combine.

Drizzle over a little balsamic vinegar to serve.

*'Who knew people would get addicted to eating raw cabbage?'*

# POACHED CHICKEN SALAD WITH ICEBERG

**SERVES 4**

*People will always order chicken salad because it's so light and easy, but they usually get palmed off with something fridge-cold, limp and dull. The secret to this salad is great chicken and a great dressing; it has to be a really good aged red wine vinegar - and don't skip the pickled currants.*

**1.4 kg (3 lb 2 oz) organic free-range chicken**
**juice of 2 lemons**
**2 tbsp currants**
**2 tbsp aged red wine vinegar**
**good pinch of chilli flakes**
**finely grated zest of 1 lemon**
**2 tbsp extra virgin olive oil**
**1/4 iceberg lettuce, shredded**
**1/2 head of radicchio or 1 treviso, trimmed, torn**
**70 g (2 1/2 oz) pine nuts, toasted**

To poach the chicken, bring a large saucepan filled with water to the boil. Add 1 teaspoon of sea salt and half the lemon juice. Rinse the chicken inside and out and add to the pan. Bring back to the boil, then simmer over low heat for 15 minutes. Remove from the heat and cover with a lid. Leave for 2 hours, allowing the residual heat to cook the chicken.

Soak the currants in the vinegar for 1 hour.

In a bowl, whisk together the chilli, lemon zest, olive oil and the remaining lemon juice. Season.

Remove the chicken from the broth (which can be saved for soup or stock). Remove the meat in large pieces, discarding the skin and bones. If the legs are not cooked through, return them to the broth and simmer for 5 minutes. Shred the chicken into long, thin strips and place in a bowl. Add the lettuce, radicchio, currant dressing and the pine nuts and gently toss to combine. Divide among bowls and serve immediately.

# CONFIT TUNA WITH BORLOTTI BEANS

**SERVES 4**

*This is such a northern Italian classic. You can confit the tuna yourself, or just pop into Fratelli Fresh and stock up on jars of Italian tuna in olive oil. Borlotti beans are in season in Australia from late spring to early winter, making this the perfect cool, lemony lunch on a sunny day.*

500 g (1 lb 2 oz) top-grade thick-cut tuna, skinned
1/2 bunch lemon thyme
2 lemons, zested, segmented (page 163)
500 ml (17 fl oz/2 cups) olive oil
500 ml (17 fl oz/2 cups) vegetable oil
250 g (9 oz) fresh borlotti (cranberry) beans, shelled
4 celery stalks, washed
1/2 bunch mint
1/2 bunch watercress
2 tbsp salted baby capers, rinsed

To confit the tuna, heat the oven to very low, about 75°C (160°F). Cut the tuna into 2.5 cm (1 in) dice. Finely chop the lemon thyme and toss with the lemon zest and freshly ground black pepper in a mixing bowl. Add the tuna and coat evenly.

Pour the two oils into an ovenproof saucepan and heat to 65°C (150°F) on a digital thermometer.

Place the tuna in the warm oil, making sure it is completely submerged. Cover and place in the oven for 20 minutes, then cool the tuna in the oil. It should still be pink when cut open. You can store the cooked tuna in the oil in the fridge for 3-4 days.

To cook the borlotti beans, place them in a saucepan of unsalted cold water and bring to the boil. Boil for 1 minute and then simmer until tender. Slice the celery on an angle.

To serve, drain the tuna, and pick and wash the mint and watercress. Toss the leaves with the celery, beans, capers and lemon segments. Arrange on a large serving platter and strew the tuna over the salad, tearing it as you go.

# BRESAOLA, RADICCHIO, APPLE & WALNUT SALAD

## SERVES 4

*There's something waldorf-y about this salad, with its crunchy apple and rich walnut components, although the wagyu bresaola (cured beef) and balsamic vinegar give it an Italian accent.*

200 g (7 oz) thinly sliced wagyu bresaola
200 g (7 oz) baby English spinach leaves
100 g (3¹/₂ oz) radicchio leaves
100 g (3¹/₂ oz) baby cos (romaine) leaves
50 g (1³/₄ oz) walnuts, toasted
1 gala apple, thinly sliced
2 tbsp lemon juice
3 tbsp extra virgin olive oil
2 tbsp aged balsamic vinegar (8 years or older)

Combine the bresaola, spinach, radicchio, cos, walnuts and apple with the lemon juice, extra virgin olive oil, sea salt and freshly ground black pepper in a large bowl.

Using salad spoons or your hands, gently toss the salad, being careful not to bruise the leaves. Divide among salad bowls or plates, and drizzle with the balsamic vinegar.

# CELERY HEART, BABY COS & ZUCCHINI FLOWERS

## SERVES 4

*The heart of the celery - the pale inner stalks with leaves - is the best part; it's very tender, not as bitter, and goes really well with cheese, which makes it extremely popular in my book. If your zucchini flowers come with small zucchinis attached, then finely slice and add them to the salad as well.*

heart from 1 bunch celery, washed
¹/₂ iceberg lettuce
1 baby cos (romaine) lettuce, trimmed
6 zucchini (courgette) flowers
4 tbsp extra virgin olive oil
juice of 1 lemon
2 tbsp chervil sprigs

Finely slice the celery heart. Tear the iceberg and cos lettuces into bite-sized pieces. Tear the petals from the zucchini flowers.

Whisk together the olive oil and lemon juice in a large bowl, and add all the ingredients, tossing well.

Season and serve immediately.

# BRUSSELS SPROUTS, PROSCIUTTO & EGG

**SERVES 4**

*Don't hate brussels sprouts. The only people who should hate brussels sprouts are people who have never shaved them finely and eaten them in a salad with prosciutto and poached eggs.*

150 g (5¹/₂ oz) brussels sprouts
¹/₂ small red (Spanish) onion, finely sliced
60 g (2¹/₄ oz) baby cavolo nero or baby spinach
1 tbsp lemon juice
3 tbsp extra virgin olive oil
6 slices prosciutto
1 tbsp white vinegar
4 or 8 very fresh eggs
50 g (1³/₄ oz) parmesan, grated
1 tbsp aged balsamic vinegar (8 years or older)

Cut the brussels sprouts in half and use a mandolin or a sharp knife to finely shave them. Place in a bowl with the onion and cavolo nero, tearing any large leaves into bite-sized pieces.

Whisk the lemon juice and extra virgin olive oil and season. Add two-thirds of the dressing to the vegetables, toss to combine and set aside for 10 minutes.

Heat the grill (broiler) to medium. Place the prosciutto on a baking tray and grill for 3 minutes or until crisp. Cool, then break into small pieces.

To poach the eggs, fill a large, deep saucepan with water and bring to a simmer, then add the vinegar. Break the eggs, one at a time, into the water and cook for 2 minutes or until the whites are set and the yolks remain runny. Use a slotted spoon to carefully remove the eggs and drain on a clean tea towel (dish towel). Trim the edges neatly.

Add the prosciutto, parmesan and remaining dressing to the salad and toss gently to combine. Divide the salad among plates, place one or two eggs on each, drizzle with the balsamic vinegar, and serve.

# OCTOPUS SALAD WITH LENTILS, POTATOES & PARSLEY

**SERVES 6**

*Octopus salad is a staple of the Mediterranean, from Italy and Greece to the south of France and Spain. They all know how to cook octopus gently and pair it sympathetically. The key is not letting the water temperature go over 90°C (195°F) or the octopus will toughen.*

100 g (3½ oz) cooking salt

1 kg (2 lb 4 oz) octopus legs/tentacles

500 ml (17 fl oz/2 cups) red wine vinegar

4 bay leaves

1 garlic bulb, cut in half crosswise

1 tbsp whole black peppercorns

500 g (1 lb 2 oz) desiree potatoes, peeled and cut into 1 cm (½ in) dice

1 kg (2 lb 4 oz) good-quality ripe tomatoes (eg ox-hearts or vine-ripened)

500 g (1 lb 2 oz) braised lentils (Basics, 253)

1 red (Spanish) onion, finely sliced

1 bunch flat-leaf parsley leaves, picked

2½ tbsp extra virgin olive oil

2 tbsp lemon juice

Prepare the brine for the octopus the day before. Dissolve the salt in 3 litres (105 fl oz/12 cups) of water, add the octopus, cover and leave for 24 hours. The following day, drain the octopus and discard the brine solution. Bring 3 litres (105 fl oz/12 cups) of water to the boil in a large saucepan. Remove from the heat and add the vinegar, bay leaves, garlic and peppercorns.

Place the octopus in the cooking liquid, and use a digital thermometer to heat to 80°C (175°F). Cook for 1½ hours or until tender.

Drain, discarding the liquid and aromatics.

Cook the potatoes in simmering, salted water for 10 minutes or until firm but cooked through. Drain and cool.

To serve, cut the octopus into 2 cm (¾ in) pieces. Cut the tomatoes into 2-3 cm (¾ in-1¼ in) dice. Combine the octopus, tomatoes, potatoes, lentils, onion and parsley in a bowl. Season and toss well with the olive oil and lemon juice.

CUCUMBER, CORNICHONS & TOASTED
BEETROOT, EGG, PINENUTS & YOGHURT
TALEGGIO & SALAD CREAM 18
PINENUTS, CURRANTS, CHILLI & MINT
PEAR, POMEGRANATES, WALNUTS &
SQUASH, ALMOND, PECORINO &
POACHED EGG & GRILLED ASPARAGUS
MIX LEAF, ASPARAGUS, PANCETTA, PATATE & PECORINO
FENNEL, AVO, CUCUMBER & SEEDED MUSTARD
AL FORNO 24
FRESH TOMATO SAUCE &
CHILLI, GARLIC & CHERRY TOMATOES
TOMATOES, BUTTER BEANS &
CHILLI, ROSEMARY & GNOCHETTI 22
CHILLI & PANGRATTATO 18
CHILLI & PANCETTA 25
MINT. PECORINO &
LENTILS &
NECK
AGRODOLCE
Fratelli Fresh

# WITLOF, GORGONZOLA & WALNUT SALAD

**SERVES 4**

*Another classic combination. The slight bitterness of the witlof, the sweetness of the pears, the crunch of the walnuts and the sharp tang of the gorgonzola make this a wham-bam of a salad.*

6 witlof (Belgian endive), finely shredded
2 corella pears, halved, cored and sliced
100 g (3$^{1}$/$_{2}$ fl oz) walnuts, roasted
150 g (5$^{1}$/$_{2}$ oz) gorgonzola piccante, roughly crumbled
$^{1}$/$_{4}$ bunch flat-leaf parsley, leaves picked
$^{1}$/$_{4}$ bunch watercress, sprigs picked
100 ml (3$^{1}$/$_{2}$ fl oz) lemon vinaigrette (Basics, 254)

Toss all the ingredients except the vinaigrette in a large bowl.

Season with sea salt (be aware the cheese can be quite salty) and freshly ground black pepper.

Dress the salad with the lemon vinaigrette and toss gently, divide among bowls and serve immediately.

———

*'Whatever we bring home from the markets we turn into a salad, whatever the season.'*

———

# SHAVED FENNEL WITH WHITE ANCHOVIES & RADISH

**SERVES 4**

*You have to have a great shaved fennel salad recipe in your life. Not just because I sell fennel, but because it's a brilliant way to eat it. White anchovies, which Italians call alici and the Spanish call boquerones, are different from the brown, salted ones. They're marinated in white wine vinegar, so they're silky, slippery and slightly sharp to the taste.*

2 fennel bulbs, tough outer layer removed
1 bunch red radishes, trimmed
50 g (1³⁄₄ oz) wild rocket (arugula)
50 g (1³⁄₄ oz) white anchovy fillets, drained
50 g (1³⁄₄ oz) parmesan, shaved
1¹⁄₂ tbsp lemon juice
3 tbsp extra virgin olive oil

Cut the fennel in half, then use a mandolin or sharp knife to thinly shave the fennel and radishes. Place the fennel and radish in a bowl with the rocket, anchovies and most of the parmesan, dress with the lemon juice and olive oil and toss gently to combine.

Spoon the salad onto a serving platter and scatter with the remaining parmesan.

# PANZANELLA WITH GOAT'S CHEESE

**SERVES 4**

*This would work with any soft cheese - even ricotta - but it's particularly good with a soft, young, fresh, tangy goat's cheese or goat's curd.*

1 kg (2 lb 4 oz) ripe ox-heart or vine-ripened tomatoes, diced
2 small red (Spanish) onions, chopped
heart from 1 bunch celery with leaves, washed, diced
1 telegraph (long) cucumber, diced
100 ml (3¹⁄₂ fl oz) extra virgin olive oil
2 tbsp aged red wine vinegar
1 tbsp lemon juice
3 thick slices day-old sourdough bread
¹⁄₂ bunch flat-leaf parsley, torn
¹⁄₂ bunch basil, leaves torn
2 tbsp salted baby capers, rinsed
200 g (7 oz) goat's cheese, crumbled

Place the tomatoes, onion, celery and cucumber in a large bowl and season lightly. Add 4 tablespoons of the olive oil, the vinegar and the lemon juice. Toss well and set aside for 20 minutes for the flavours to develop.

Heat the oven to 180°C (350°F). Tear the bread into small, bite-sized chunks, brush with the remaining olive oil and bake for 10 minutes or until dry and golden.

Five minutes before serving, toss the bread with the salad to let it soften a little. Just before serving, add parsley, basil, capers and goat's cheese, season well and toss gently to combine. Serve immediately.

# SMOKED TROUT WITH ASPARAGUS & EGG

**SERVES 4**

*Asparagus and soft-boiled eggs - so good. Add smoked trout, and you have an instant salad for a weekend brunch or midweek dinner that is a lot more special than it has to be.*

350 g (12 oz) smoked river trout
2 bunches asparagus, woody ends removed
4 eggs
1/4 bunch dill, chopped
juice of 1 lemon
100 ml (3 1/2 fl oz) mayonnaise
120 g (4 1/4 oz/3 cups) mixed salad leaves

Remove the skin and bones from the trout and discard. Gently flake the flesh into a bowl.

Bring a saucepan of salted water to the boil. Cut the asparagus in half and blanch for 2–3 minutes or until tender. Drain and refresh in cold water.

Gently place the eggs in boiling water and boil for 5 1/2 minutes. Use a slotted spoon to remove the eggs from the water and cool in iced water. Peel the eggs under cold running water and set aside.

Mix the dill, lemon juice and mayonnaise together in a bowl and season with sea salt.

Toss the smoked trout, mixed leaves, asparagus and dill mayonnaise together in a bowl.

Divide between shallow bowls. Cut the soft-boiled eggs in half and arrange two halves on each salad. Scatter with freshly ground black pepper and serve.

CASSATA - CANDIED ORANGE

BACI DI DAMA

# Dolce e Gelati

MANGOES IN MOSCATO

CAMPARI & ORANGE

TIRAMISU

VANILLA BEAN GELATO

ORANGE GELATO

GELATO

# CANNOLI WITH ORANGE MASCARPONE

## SERVES 4

*Cannoli are big on crunch, big on cream - the perfect vehicle for the season's best fruits. If you don't have stainless-steel cannoli tubes to help form the shape, then tubes of dried cannelloni pasta work just as well.*

### CANNOLI SHELLS
**MAKES 20**

80 g (2¾ oz) unsalted butter, chopped

380 g (13½ oz) plain (all-purpose) flour, plus extra for dusting

1 egg

2 egg yolks

70 g (2½ oz) icing (confectioners') sugar

100 ml (3½ fl oz) Marsala

oil, for deep-frying

### ORANGE MASCARPONE

250 g (9 oz) mascarpone

250 g (9 oz) fresh ricotta

3 tbsp icing (confectioners') sugar, plus extra to serve

zest of 2 oranges

1 tsp Grand Marnier

### STRAWBERRIES IN PROSECCO

½ vanilla bean, split

375 ml (13 fl oz/1½ cups) prosecco

200 g (7 oz) caster (superfine) sugar

500 g (1 lb 2 oz) punnets strawberries, hulled

To poach the strawberries, scrape the seeds from the vanilla bean and add to the prosecco with 150 ml (5 fl oz) of water and the sugar. Bring to the boil over medium heat and boil until reduced by half. Remove from the heat, add the strawberries and leave to cool.

To make the orange mascarpone, use a spatula to gently combine all the ingredients then refrigerate.

To make the cannoli shells, rub the butter and flour together with your fingers until roughly combined, then place in the bowl of an electric mixer with a dough hook attachment. Add the whole egg and the yolks, icing sugar and Marsala and knead in the machine until it forms a dough. Remove from the bowl, cut into five pieces and wrap in plastic wrap. Refrigerate overnight.

Put the dough through a pasta machine until it is 1 mm (1⁄32 in) thick. Place on a floured bench and cut into 10 cm (4 in) diameter circles. Brush the top edge of each circle with egg yolk and wrap around a cannoli or stainless steel tube to form a tubular shape.

Remove from the mould and set aside.

Heat the oil in a deep-fryer to 140°C (275°F). Deep-fry the shells for 5-6 minutes or until cooked through. Remove and allow to cool on paper towel.

When ready to eat, pipe the orange mascarpone into each cannoli shell. Place a spoonful of strawberries and some syrup in each shallow bowl, add the cannoli, dust with icing sugar and serve.

# BACI DI DAMA

**MAKES 12**

*These sweet little 'ladies' kisses' from the Piemonte region can be made with hazelnuts or almonds, or a mix of both. If you're a Nutella freak, use it instead of dark chocolate to sandwich them together.*

110 g (3¾ oz) granulated sugar
150 g (5½ oz) blanched almonds
150 g (5½ oz) unsalted butter, softened
150 g (5½ oz) plain (all-purpose) flour
1 vanilla bean, split
zest of 1 large orange
150 g (5½ oz) dark (70%) chocolate, chopped

Place the sugar and almonds in a food processor and blend until they form fine crumbs.

Combine the butter, flour and the almond mixture in a heavy-duty food processor fitted with a paddle attachment and process until smooth.

Scrape out the little black seeds of the vanilla bean and add to the mixture with the orange zest and a pinch of sea salt and process until it forms a smooth dough, then remove from the bowl and roll into a log approximately 5 cm (2 in) wide. Wrap in plastic wrap and refrigerate for 2 hours or until firm.

Heat the oven to 160°C (325°F). Cut the dough into 24 pieces, about 10 g (¼ oz) each. Roll into balls, place on a greased baking tray and bake for 20 minutes. Remove from the oven and allow to cool.

Meanwhile, melt the chocolate in a heatproof bowl over a saucepan of gently simmering water - make sure the water is not touching the bottom of the bowl - until smooth. Set aside for 5 minutes to cool slightly.

To assemble, spoon a little of the melted chocolate on half the biscuits, place another biscuit on top and gently press them together.

Refrigerate for 20-30 minutes before serving, or store in an airtight container in the fridge for up to 1 week.

# CHOCOLATE BUDINO

**SERVES 4**

*A gorgeous chocolatey pudding that should be served with lashings of cream or ice cream or both.*

1 tbsp melted butter
200 g (7 oz) unsalted butter, softened
200 g (7 oz) dark (70%) chocolate, chopped
4 eggs
4 egg yolks
200 g (7 oz) caster (superfine) sugar
100 g (3½ oz) plain (all-purpose) flour, sifted
icing (confectioners') sugar, for dusting

Place 4 x 150 ml (5 fl oz) ramekins in the fridge to cool for 20 minutes. Remove and brush the ramekins with the melted butter and return to the fridge.

Place the butter and chocolate in a large bowl and place over a gently simmering saucepan of water until melted and smooth. Set aside to cool to room temperature.

Heat the oven to 190°C (375°F). In a food processor or electric mixer, beat the whole eggs, yolks and sugar until the mixture forms white ribbons when lifted. Add the flour and beat until well combined. Pour the cooled melted chocolate into the mixture and combine.

Remove the ramekins from the fridge and fill with the mixture.

Bake for 12-13 minutes or until set. Gently invert the ramekins onto warm plates, dust with icing sugar and serve.

# CASSATA WITH CANDIED ORANGE

## SERVES 8–10

*Cassata doesn't always refer to ice cream; sometimes it means this amazing Sicilian dessert of ricotta, dried fruit and almonds instead. Here, it's built on an internal structure of Italian panettone cake.*

1 kg (2 lb 4 oz) panettone

1 kg (2 lb 4 oz) dry ricotta

200 g (7 oz) mixed peel

185 g (6½ oz) toasted blanched almonds, roughly chopped

330 g (11¾ oz) caster (superfine) sugar

100 ml (3½ fl oz) Cointreau

1 orange

500 g (1 lb 2 oz) dark (70%) chocolate, roughly chopped

200 g (7 oz) butter, chopped

'The best desserts are based on fresh, seasonal fruit. And chocolate.'

Line a 25 cm x 10 cm x 10 cm (10 in x 4 in x 4 in) loaf tin with plastic wrap, leaving enough overhang to cover the tin. Slice the panettone into 1 cm (½ in) thick slices. Combine the ricotta with the mixed peel, almonds, 110 g (3¾ oz) of the sugar and half the Cointreau.

Layer one slice of panettone in the base of the loaf tin and drizzle with a little of the remaining Cointreau. Add one layer of the ricotta mix. Repeat twice more, finishing with one layer of panettone. Cover with the overhanging plastic wrap, ensuring everything is tightly enclosed. Overturn the loaf tin on to a chopping board and refrigerate for 2 hours or longer.

Use a vegetable peeler or a sharp knife to remove the peel from the orange, ensuring most of the white pith is removed from the peel. Slice the orange peel into 2 mm (1/16 in) wide strips. Bring 500 ml (17 fl oz/2 cups) water to the boil, add the remaining 220 g (7¾ oz) sugar and stir until dissolved. Add the orange peel and simmer until the liquid is reduced by half. Cool the liquid and the orange peel to room temperature.

When the panettone loaf is set, melt the chocolate and butter in a heatproof bowl set over a saucepan of simmering water, making sure the bowl isn't touching the water.

Remove the panettone loaf from the tin and remove the plastic wrap. Coat all sides of the panettone loaf with an even layer of warm chocolate, reserving enough to coat the base. Put the panettone loaf back in the fridge to set the chocolate, and keep the remaining chocolate warm. When set, turn the panettone loaf over and coat the bottom, then return to the fridge to set. Once set, trim any untidy edges.

To serve, thickly slice the panettone loaf with a warm knife. Scatter with the orange peel and drizzle with the orange syrup.

# FIG & ALMOND TART

**SERVES 6**

*Fresh figs are so magnificent we try to come up with different ways of enjoying them every year. While they are a seasonal fruit, our growers have extended the season with beautiful-quality fruit for months either side of summer.*

**1 quantity sweet shortcrust pastry (Basics, 259)**
**100 g (3¹/₂ oz) raspberry or apricot jam**
**6 fresh figs, sliced**
**vanilla bean gelato (page 243), to serve**

**FRANGIPANE**
**250 g (9 oz) unsalted butter**
**250 g (9 oz) caster (superfine) sugar**
**4 eggs**
**110 g (3³/₄ oz) plain (all-purpose) flour**
**250 g (9 oz) almond meal**

Heat the oven to 200°C (400°F). Line 6 small loose-based flan (tart) tins with the pastry, and cover the bases with a thin layer of jam.

To make the frangipane filling, use electric beaters to cream the butter and sugar until pale, about 5 minutes. Add the eggs one by one. If you add them too fast, the mixture will split. If this happens, add a little of the almond meal.

Once the eggs are combined, add the flour and almond meal and mix until combined. Scrape into a piping bag and pipe into the tart shells. Gently push the figs slightly into the frangipane and bake for 20-30 minutes or until the tarts are golden and cooked through. Allow to cool slightly before removing from the tins.

Serve warm or at room temperature with vanilla bean gelato.

# CREMA DEL' AMARETTO

**SERVES 4**

*Amaretto is a sweet, almond-flavoured Italian liqueur, well worth having to hand for those moments you need a heart-warming digestivo after dinner, either straight or on the rocks.*

**600 ml (21 fl oz) thickened (whipping) cream**
**6 egg yolks (140 g/5 oz in total)**
**100 g (3¹/₂ oz) caster (superfine) sugar,**
  **plus 2 tbsp extra**
**2¹/₂ tbsp amaretto**

Heat the oven to 120°C (250°F). In a saucepan, heat the cream to a simmer (do not boil). In a large bowl, whisk the egg yolks and sugar until the sugar has just dissolved. Gradually whisk the cream into the egg mixture. Whisk in the amaretto, and strain the mixture through a fine sieve, skimming any bubbles off the surface. Pour into 4 x 180 ml (6 fl oz) ramekins.

Place a folded tea towel (dish towel) in the base of a roasting tin and place the ramekins on top. Add boiling water to the tin until it comes halfway up the sides of the ramekins. Bake for 45 minutes or until almost set. Remove and cool for 1 hour, then cover and refrigerate overnight.

To serve, cover the tops with the extra sugar and caramelise with a brulee torch.

# MANGOES IN MOSCATO

**SERVES 4**

*Moscato is a sweet, lightly sparkling Italian dessert wine. You could use a late-harvest dessert wine instead, and throw in any berries, from strawberries to blueberries, you like.*

2 mangoes
500 g (1 lb 2 oz) strawberries
2 tsp caster (superfine) sugar
finely grated zest of 1/2 lemon
375 ml (13 fl oz/11/2 cups) chilled moscato

**CHANTILLY CREAM**
150 ml (5 fl oz) thin (pouring) cream
2 tbsp icing (confectioners') sugar
1/2 vanilla bean, split

To make the chantilly cream, place the cream in a bowl, sift the icing sugar over, then scrape in the tiny black seeds of the vanilla bean on top. Use electric beaters or a hand whisk to beat the cream to soft peaks. Refrigerate until needed.

Cut two large cheeks from each mango, and cut the flesh into 1.5 cm (5/8 in) dice, without cutting through the skin. Turn each cheek inside out and cut off the protruding cubes of mango, discarding the skin. Hull the strawberries and cut in half.

Combine the mango, strawberries, sugar and lemon zest in a bowl and lightly toss. Spoon the fruit among serving glasses and put 3-4 tablespoons moscato into each glass. Top with the chantilly cream and serve.

# CHOCOLATE & NOUGAT SEMIFREDDO

**SERVES 4**

*The French have their parfait and the Italians have their semifreddo, which means semi-frozen. This is a stunning dessert for entertaining because you can make it ahead and just slice it to serve. Its beauty rests on sensational nougat and great chocolate.*

3 egg yolks
50 g (13/4 oz) caster (superfine) sugar
250 ml (9 fl oz/1 cup) thickened (whipping) cream
1 tbsp rum
100 g (31/2 oz) dark (70%) chocolate, chopped
100 g (31/2 oz) hard nougat, chopped
2 egg whites
extra dark (70%) chocolate, grated or shaved, to serve

Line a greased terrine mould with two layers of plastic wrap, leaving some extra hanging over the sides to cover the top.

Use electric beaters to beat the egg yolks and sugar until pale.

In a bowl, whisk the cream until semi-firm, then fold in the rum. Gently fold the yolk mixture into the cream, then gently fold in the chocolate and nougat.

In a bowl, whisk the egg whites to stiff peaks and fold through the mixture.

Pour into the lined mould, cover with plastic wrap and freeze overnight.

To serve, unwrap the semifreddo and turn onto a chopping board. Use a hot knife to cut thick slices or wedges and serve with grated or shaved chocolate.

# WHITE CHOCOLATE BAVARESE

**SERVES 4**

*Bavarese is the Italian way of saying 'bavarois', which in turn is the French way of saying 'Bavarian', which is all a bit complicated, but at least it makes you appreciate why the EU is in the mess it's in. You can serve these with the strawberries in prosecco (page 216).*

4 gelatine sheets
80 g (2¾ oz) caster (superfine) sugar
3 egg yolks
1 vanilla bean, split
300 ml (10½ fl oz) milk
140 g (5 oz) white chocolate, grated
330 ml (11¼ fl oz/1⅓ cups) thickened
  (whipping) cream

Soak the gelatine in a bowl of cold water until it is soft (about 4 minutes), then drain and squeeze out the excess water.

Beat the sugar and egg yolks in a heavy-duty food processor or electric mixer until the sugar has dissolved and the mixture becomes creamy.

Scrape the little black vanilla seeds from the vanilla bean into the milk and bring to the boil over medium heat. Add a small amount of the hot milk to the sugar mixture and stir well, then add the remaining hot milk, the gelatine and the chocolate. Leave the mixture to cool to room temperature.

Whip the cream until firm peaks form, then gently fold through the chocolate mixture.

Pour into 4 x 150 ml (5 fl oz) moulds and refrigerate for at least 3 hours before serving.

# TORTA DI BANOFFEE

**SERVES 10–12**

*Founding Café Sopra chef Andy Bunn introduced this banana and toffee dessert from his childhood – which was great, apart from the fact that his childhood was in Yorkshire, not in Italy.*

2 x 395 g (13¾ oz) tins sweetened condensed milk
185 g (6½ oz) unsalted butter, chopped
375 g (13 oz) digestive biscuits, halved
2 vanilla beans, split
600 ml (21 fl oz) thickened (whipping) cream
75 g (2¾ oz) icing (confectioners') sugar, sifted
4 bananas
30 g (1 oz) dark (70%) chocolate, finely grated

Place the two unopened tins of condensed milk in large saucepan, cover with water and bring to the boil over medium heat. Reduce the heat and simmer for 3 hours, adding more water when necessary to ensure the tins remain covered. Remove the tins and cool in the fridge for 2 hours.

Meanwhile, melt the butter in a small saucepan and cool slightly.

Use a food processor to process the biscuits to fine crumbs, then add the melted butter and process briefly to combine. Press the crumb mixture over the base of a greased 28 cm (11¼ in) loose-based flan (tart) tin, then refrigerate for 30 minutes to firm up.

Open the cooled cans of condensed milk, and spoon the caramel evenly over the biscuit base, then refrigerate overnight to firm.

Scrape the little black vanilla seeds into the cream. Use electric beaters to whisk the cream, vanilla and sugar to stiff peaks. Cut the bananas into thin slices. Gently remove the sides of the tart tin, and place the tart base on a cake stand or flat plate. Spoon or pipe half the cream over the caramel filling, then place the bananas in slightly overlapping concentric circles, working from the outside in.

Top with the remaining cream, scatter with the chocolate and serve immediately.

# TORTA DELLA NONNA

**SERVES 12**

*In Tuscany, all the best meals end with a thin wedge of this generously large and deliciously rich custard-filled 'grandmother's' tart.*

750 g (1 lb 10 oz) plain (all-purpose) flour
375 g (13 oz) unsalted butter, softened
210 g (7½ oz) icing (confectioners') sugar
6 egg yolks

**FILLING**

1 litre (35 fl oz/4 cups) milk
10 egg yolks
220 g (7¾ oz) caster (superfine) sugar
100 g (3½ oz) plain (all-purpose) flour
150 ml (5 fl oz) lemon juice
4 tbsp toasted flaked almonds

To make the pastry, process the flour and butter in a food processor to fine crumbs, then pulse in the sugar and egg yolks. Turn out the mixture onto a clean bench and bring together by hand. Wrap in plastic wrap and rest in the fridge for 1 hour.

Roll out the pastry between two layers of plastic wrap until 5 mm (¼ in) thick. Cover the base and sides of a 25 cm (10 in) diameter loose-based flan (tart) tin with the pastry. Set aside in a cool place to rest.

Heat the oven to 150°C (300°F).

To make the filling, bring the milk to the boil over medium heat, then set aside. Meanwhile, in a large bowl, use a hand whisk to whisk the egg yolks and sugar together until smooth, then slowly add the flour, whisking until combined. Slowly pour about 125 ml (4 fl oz/½ cup) of the hot milk into the egg mixture, whisking constantly. Pour the mixture back into the saucepan, then cook over low heat, whisking constantly, for 5 minutes or until it is thick enough to coat the back of a spoon.

Whisk in the lemon juice, pour the mixture into the tart case and bake for 45 minutes or until just set. Allow to cool to room temperature. Scatter with the almonds and serve.

# TIRAMISU

SERVES 6

*It's a classic for a reason. Coffee, booze and mascarpone combine to make one of Italy's most famous desserts.*

100 g (3½ oz) caster (superfine) sugar
150 ml (5 fl oz) freshly made espresso coffee
1½ tbsp dark rum
240 ml (8 fl oz) sweet Marsala
3 eggs, separated
750 g (1 lb 10 oz) mascarpone
150 g (5½ oz) savoiardi biscuits or sliced, stale panettone
20 g (¾ oz) dark (70%) chocolate, finely grated

To make the coffee soaking mixture, stir 30 g (1 oz) of the sugar into the hot espresso until dissolved, then stir in the rum and 185 ml (6 fl oz) of the Marsala. Set aside to cool.

Use electric beaters to whisk together the egg yolks and the remaining sugar. Add the remaining Marsala, then whisk in the mascarpone until smooth, taking care not to over-beat it.

Use electric beaters to whisk the egg whites to stiff peaks, then gently fold into the mascarpone mixture.

To assemble, spread a quarter of the mascarpone mixture over the base of an 11 cm x 23 cm (4¼ in x 9 in), 9 cm/3½ in deep plastic, glass or stainless-steel dish or container.

Dip the savoiardi biscuits one at a time into the coffee mixture, allowing them to soak up some liquid, then layer six of them over the cream. Repeat this layering twice more with the mascarpone mixture and soaked biscuits, then finish with the remaining quarter of mascarpone mixture over the top. Refrigerate for 4 hours or overnight.

Scatter the chocolate over the top and serve.

# PANETTONE BREAD & BUTTER PUDDING

**SERVES 6**

*Once you have made bread and butter pudding with panettone, that lovely light, yeasty Italian cake, you'll never go back to using plain, everyday bread.*

80 g (2³/₄ oz) dried muscatels
4 tbsp sweet Marsala
1 kg (2 lb 4 oz) panettone
4 eggs
2 egg yolks
80 g (2³/₄ oz) caster (superfine) sugar
600 ml (21 fl oz) thin (pouring) cream
1¹/₂ tbsp honey
icing (confectioners') sugar, for dusting
100 g (3¹/₂ oz) mascarpone, to serve (optional)

Heat the oven to 180°C (350°F). Place the muscatels and Marsala in a small saucepan and simmer for 3-5 minutes or until the muscatels are softened and the Marsala is reduced and syrupy. Cool.

Trim the crust from the panettone and cut into quarters, then cut each quarter into 1.5 cm (⁵/₈ in) thick slices, a little smaller than a slice of bread. Arrange the slices in a single layer in a greased 23 cm (9 in) square ovenproof dish. Scatter with half the muscatels, then top with another layer of panettone and the remaining muscatels.

Pour any remaining Marsala into a bowl, add the eggs, egg yolks and caster sugar and whisk until combined, then whisk in the cream. Pour the mixture over the panettone, then drizzle over the honey.

Place the dish in a deep roasting tin and pour in enough hot water to reach halfway up the sides. Bake for 35 minutes or until the custard is just set. Remove the dish from the water bath and stand for 10 minutes.

Dust with icing sugar, top with a spoonful of mascarpone (if using), and serve warm or at room temperature.

# PISTACHIO PANNA COTTA WITH CRANBERRY JELLY

**SERVES 4**

*Shivery, milky-white panna cotta meets shaky, fruity, ruby-red jelly in a new spin on everyone's favourite dessert.*

**2 gelatine sheets**
**750 ml (26 fl oz/3 cups) thin (pouring) cream**
**120 g (4¼ oz) caster (superfine) sugar**
**150 ml (5 fl oz) milk**
**80 g (2¾ oz) pistachio nuts, finely ground**

**JELLY**
**1½ gelatine sheets**
**250 ml (9 fl oz/1 cup) cranberry juice**
**100 g (3½ oz) caster (superfine) sugar**
**1 tsp vanilla extract**
**8 raspberries**
**8 blueberries**
**8 strawberries**

To make the jelly, soak the gelatine in a bowl of cold water until it is soft (about 4 minutes), then drain and squeeze out the excess water.

Meanwhile, heat the cranberry juice, sugar and vanilla in a saucepan over medium heat, stirring until the sugar has melted. Allow to cool slightly then add the gelatine and stir to combine.

Distribute the berries between four tall dessert glasses and pour in the jelly mix. Refrigerate until set.

To make the panna cotta, soak the gelatine in a bowl of cold water until it is soft (about 4 minutes), then drain and squeeze out the excess water.

Bring the cream, sugar and milk to the boil in a medium saucepan over medium heat, then allow to cool for 5 minutes. Add the gelatine and pistachios, mixing well. Allow to cool to room temperature (if too hot, it will melt the jelly). Spoon the panna cotta mixture into the glasses over the jelly, and return to the fridge for at least 4 hours, then serve.

# TORTA DI VERONA

**SERVES 8**

*This exquisite dessert has charmed Sydneysiders since it first appeared on the menu at a modern Italian restaurant called Taylor's. It's based on the traditional pandoro, or golden bread, of Verona, and is almost like brioche in its rich, soft crumb and light, buttery flavour. The classic panettone is easier to find and gives a beautiful result.*

8 eggs, separated
1 kg (2 lb 4 oz) mascarpone
475 g (1 lb 1 oz) caster (superfine) sugar
150 ml (5 fl oz) sweet Marsala
150 ml (5 fl oz) amaretto
750 g (1 lb 10 oz) panettone or brioche
120 g (4¼ oz) flaked almonds
250 g (9 oz) blueberries
2 tsp lemon juice

Use electric beaters to whisk the egg yolks, mascarpone and 150 g (5½ oz) of the sugar to stiff peaks. In a clean bowl, whisk the egg whites to soft peaks. Slowly add 150 g (5½ oz) of the sugar and whisk to stiff peaks. Use a metal spoon to fold one-third of the whites into the mascarpone to loosen, then fold in the remainder.

Combine the Marsala and amaretto in a bowl. Remove the crusts from the panettone, then slice horizontally into eight. Place half the slices over the base of a 23 cm x 29 cm (9 in x 11½ in), 3.5 litre (118 fl oz/14 cup) dish. Brush with half the alcohol and spread over half the mascarpone. Repeat with the remaining panettone, alcohol and mascarpone. Refrigerate for 3-4 hours.

To make the croccante (toffee almonds), heat the oven to 160°C (325°F). In a small saucepan, stir 20 g (¾ oz) of the sugar into 3 tablespoons of water over low heat until it dissolves, then simmer until syrupy. Combine the almonds and 55 g (2 oz) of the sugar in a bowl. Drizzle the syrup over the almonds, mixing well and ensuring there are no clumps of sugar. Spread over a baking paper-lined tray and bake for 15 minutes, stirring halfway, or until golden and crisp, then allow to cool.

Heat a heavy-based saucepan over medium heat. Add the blueberries, lemon juice and the remaining 100 g (3½ oz) of sugar. Stir until the juice begins to run, then cook for 2 minutes or until syrupy; the berries should still hold their shape. Set aside to cool.

To serve, scatter the torta with the toffee almonds, divide among bowls and drizzle with the blueberry sauce.

# TANGELO & POLENTA CAKE

**SERVES 6–8**

*Polenta started life as yellow maize flour that made a nourishing, creamy, golden meal for the poor and the workers. Here, it gets a bit of a leg-up in the class department in a lovely cake scented with vibrant tangelo, a tangy hybrid of the tangerine and the grapefruit.*

4 tangelos, zested
450 g (1 lb) unsalted butter, at room temperature, plus a little extra for greasing
550 g (1 lb 4 oz) caster (superfine) sugar
6 eggs
1 vanilla bean, split
450 g (1 lb) almond meal
225 g (8 oz) instant polenta (cornmeal)
1 tsp baking powder

Heat the oven to 165°C (325°F). Lightly grease a 30 cm (12 in) diameter spring-form cake tin and line with baking paper.

Juice two of the zested tangelos, then slice the remaining two.

Use the paddle of an electric beater to cream the butter and 450 g (1 lb) of the sugar for about 5 minutes or until pale. Add the eggs, one at a time, making sure each is combined before adding the next.

Scrape in the seeds of the vanilla bean, and slowly beat in the tangelo zest and one-quarter of the tangelo juice.

Lastly, add the almond meal, polenta, baking powder and a pinch of sea salt. Once combined, pour the mixture into the cake tin and bake for 1 hour 15 minutes or until a thin bamboo skewer inserted into the cake comes out clean.

Meanwhile, combine the remaining sugar with the sliced tangelos and the remaining tangelo juice in a small, non-reactive saucepan. Bring to the boil and cook for 10 minutes or until syrupy.

Pour the hot syrup over the cake while it is still in its tin, and allow to cool.

Cut into big wedges to serve.

# CHOCOLATE TORTE

**SERVES 10**

*Chocolate, as we know, is one of the five essential food groups. And this is the ultimate chocolate dessert: rich, dark and satisfying. Even people who don't like dessert like this one because it's just so pure. Serve it with fresh berries or cream, or both.*

5 eggs
280 g (10 oz) caster (superfine) sugar
300 g (10½ oz) dark (70%) chocolate, chopped
115 g (4 oz) unsalted butter, softened

Spray a 28 cm x 8 cm (11¼ in x 3¼ in) terrine mould or loaf tin with cooking oil, and line with baking paper.

In a heavy-duty food processor or electric mixer, beat the eggs and 80 g (2¾ oz) of the sugar until white and creamy.

Bring 125 ml (4 fl oz/½ cup) of water and the remaining sugar to the boil over medium heat until the sugar has dissolved.

Heat the oven to 165°C (325°F).

Stir the chocolate and butter in a heatproof bowl over a saucepan of simmering water until melted and smooth, then remove from the heat. Add the sugar syrup and stir to combine, then add the egg mixture and fold together. Pour into the mould.

Place a clean, folded tea towel (dish towel) on the base of a baking tin, and place the mould on top. Pour hot water into the tray until it comes about 2.5 cm (1 in) up the sides of the mould. Bake for 45 minutes or until set.

Remove the torte from the oven (do not unmould) and allow to cool, then place in the fridge for 5 hours. To unmould, invert onto a serving plate and remove the baking paper. Cut into slices and serve.

# GELATO

Australians love gelato almost as much as Italians do, because we've grown up with the real thing - artisanal Italian gelato and sorbetto.

There is a big difference between the two. Gelato is more like ice cream, using milk, cream or a custard base, making it dense and silky. Sorbetti are dairy-free and egg-free, usually just made with pure fruit and a simple sugar syrup, and churned until soft and snowy.

Like its Italian cousins, pizza and pasta, the best gelato is made with very few ingredients, and those ingredients have to be very fresh, very recognisable and of the highest quality.

Everyone goes for the old-school vanilla, chocolate, stracciatella (chocolate chip) and tiramisu flavours in gelato, whereas sorbetto is such a brilliant carrier of flavour you can start with something very simple and pure, like a mango, raspberry or white nectarine, and it will still be magnificent.

Many people don't realise that both gelati and sorbetti can be as seasonal as anything else you eat. Depending on the season, we use melons, oranges and lemons, and nuts such as pistachio. Liqueurs such as amaretto and limoncello, espresso coffee, and fresh, light cheeses such as mascarpone and ricotta are also great choices throughout the year.

Then there's the classic affogato dessert, where you drown vanilla bean ice cream in freshly made, hot espresso coffee, until it all melts into a hot/cold, bitter/sweet puddle of wonderment. To make it, place two small scoops of gelato in six glasses or espresso cups and return to the freezer. Make six double shots of espresso, pour the espresso over the top - and a shot of amaretto or nocello as well, if you like - and serve immediately.

And don't forget to make sgroppino cocktails if you have a tub of lemon gelato in the freezer: just add scoops of lemon gelato to chilled glasses, and slowly pour in some very chilled sparkling wine, which will froth up and bubble.

## MASCARPONE GELATO

### SERVES 6

*This is one of the nicest, richest, creamiest gelati ever made, because you are starting with mascarpone, and not just cream, milk or custard. It is gorgeous on its own or served with the raspberry sorbetto (page 240) as well.*

**400 g (14 oz) caster (superfine) sugar**
**500 g (1 lb 2 oz) mascarpone**
**125 ml (4 fl oz/1/2 cup) lemon juice**

To make the sugar syrup, combine 400 ml (14 fl oz) of water and the sugar in a saucepan over medium heat. Bring to the boil, stirring, and simmer until the sugar has dissolved. Cool, then refrigerate until cold.

Place the mascarpone in a large bowl and slowly whisk in the cold sugar syrup until combined. Add the lemon juice, whisking, and churn in an ice cream maker until thick and frozen. Transfer to an airtight container and freeze until ready to serve.

If you don't have an ice cream maker, you can still make beautiful gelato or sorbetto by freezing the mixture in a shallow container for 1 hour, then removing it and breaking up the crystals with a fork. Repeat this another two or three times and you will have a nice, smooth, melt-in-the-mouth result.

# CAMPARI & ORANGE GELATO

**SERVES 6**

*If it's good to drink as a cocktail, it's good to eat as gelato (pictured right), we say.*

250 g (9 oz) caster (superfine) sugar
500 ml (17 fl oz/2 cups) strained orange juice
juice of 1 lime
4 tbsp Campari
2 egg whites, whisked

To make the sugar syrup, combine 200 ml (7 fl oz) of water and the sugar in a saucepan and stir over low heat until the sugar dissolves. Bring to the boil, then reduce the heat and simmer, uncovered, for 5 minutes. Add the orange juice, lime juice and Campari and stir over low heat until combined. Churn in an ice cream maker until almost frozen. Add the egg whites, and continue churning until combined, then freeze until ready to serve.

Serve scoops of Campari and orange gelato in glasses. Alternatively, save the oranges you have juiced, clean all the flesh and pith from each half-shell and divide the freshly churned gelato between the shells. Smooth the top and freeze. To serve, place cut-side down on a board and use a serrated knife to cut into wedges.

# RASPBERRY SORBETTO

**SERVES 4**

*The best way to serve this berry-pink, dairy-free sorbetto is with more berries.*

175 g (6 oz) caster (superfine) sugar
80 g (2³⁄₄ oz) liquid glucose
250 g (9 oz) fresh raspberries
1 tbsp lemon juice

To make the sugar syrup, heat 400 ml (14 fl oz) of water, the sugar and liquid glucose in a saucepan over medium heat until the sugar has dissolved. Set aside and allow to cool in the fridge.

Once cooled, use a blender or stick blender to process the raspberries and lemon juice with the sugar syrup until smooth, then pass through a fine sieve, scraping with a rubber spatula to extract as much juice as possible. Churn in an ice cream maker until thick and frozen. Spoon the mixture into an airtight container and freeze for 4 hours or until ready to serve.

# VANILLA BEAN GELATO

**SERVES 6**

*Everyone's favourite from the very first lick; this is the classic, much-loved, custard-based vanilla bean gelato.*

250 ml (9 fl oz/1 cup) thin (pouring) cream
250 ml (9 fl oz/1 cup) milk
1 vanilla bean, split
110 g (3¾ oz) caster (superfine) sugar
5 egg yolks

Combine the cream, milk, vanilla bean and scraped-out seeds in a heavy-based saucepan and slowly bring to a slow simmer over low-medium heat. Set aside.

Meanwhile, whisk the sugar and egg yolks in a bowl for about 2 minutes or until thick and pale. Gradually whisk in a little of the warm cream mixture, then gradually whisk the egg yolk mixture into the remaining warm cream.

Cook over low heat, stirring constantly with a wooden spoon, until the custard is thick enough to coat the back of the spoon. Do not allow to boil. Strain through a fine sieve into a bowl placed over another bowl filled with ice and cool, stirring occasionally. Churn in an ice cream maker, then transfer to an airtight container and freeze until ready to serve.

# CIOCCOLATO GELATO

**SERVES 6**

*Smooth, dark and velvety, this is a very grown-up gelato, as good in a cone as in an affogato.*

600 ml (21 fl oz) milk
250 ml (9 fl oz/1 cup) thickened (whipping) cream
1 tbsp cornflour (cornstarch)
200 g (7 oz) caster (superfine) sugar
150 g (5½ oz) dark (70%) chocolate, finely chopped

Place 2 tablespoons of the milk and 2 tablespoons of the cream in a small bowl, add the cornflour and whisk until smooth. Set aside.

Place the remaining milk and cream in a saucepan and add the sugar. Bring to the boil over medium heat. Once boiled, add the cornflour mixture and cook for about 1 minute, stirring constantly. Remove from the heat and add the chocolate, stirring until melted and combined. Strain through a fine sieve into a bowl sitting on another bowl filled with ice, to help it cool. Refrigerate for 4 hours, then churn in an ice cream maker until thick and frozen. Spoon into an airtight container and freeze for 4 hours or until ready to serve.

# CONSERVE DEL PADRE

My father, Tom, could start a fan club for his jams. They've been a regular feature of our business since he started helping us sort the fruit at the wholesale fruit and vegetable market more than 20 years ago. A lot of ripe apricots were going to be tossed, so he asked if he could take them home and turn them into jam.

I should point out that, at that stage, he had never actually made a jar of jam in his life. But he threw himself into it, and that very first batch of apricot jam was surprisingly good, apart from the fact that the jars subsequently started to explode in the cupboards.

So he learnt a bit more about the finer points of jam-making, stocked up on *Women's Weekly* cookbooks, and soon got it down pat. It's a good feeling to have those beautiful jars on the shelf, preserving what can be quite delicate and seasonal; fruit that wouldn't otherwise last very long - mind you, he has gone through three stoves in the process.

It makes him the perfect person to ask for a few tips on jams and jam-making, so here they are:

'Good, just-ripe fruit is the key. Without that, you'll never get a great jam.

'There are three important things to remember: how to sterilise your jars, how to test if your jam is done, and not to wander off to answer the phone halfway through. To sterilise your jars, heat the oven to 100°C (200°F). Rinse the jars and lids in boiling water. Place the jars upside-down on baking trays in the oven until completely dry. Dry the lids thoroughly with paper towel.

'To test if your jam is done, place a teaspoonful of it on a saucer and freeze it for 4 minutes. If it's thick and wrinkles when you push it, it's done. If it's thin and runny, keep cooking.

'Finally, enjoy the fruits of your labours. My favourite breakfast is beautiful fresh bread, slathered with my own apricot jam. And always make too much, so you can give some away. People love it.'

## APRICOT JAM
### MAKES ABOUT 1.25 LITRES (44 FL OZ/5 CUPS)

1 kg (2 lb 4 oz) apricots
900 g (2 lb) granulated sugar

Cut the apricots in half, reserving half the stones. Wrap the stones in a clean tea towel (dish towel) and crack with a hammer. Extract the kernels, discarding the stones. Blanch the kernels in boiling water for 1 minute, then drain, peel and split in two.

Place the apricots and 300 ml (10½ fl oz) water in a large saucepan and bring to the boil. Simmer for about 15 minutes or until the fruit is soft. Add the sugar and kernels to the pan and simmer gently, stirring, until the sugar has dissolved.

Bring the mixture to the boil and allow to boil, uncovered, without stirring, for about 15 minutes or until a teaspoon of the jam sets to your liking when placed on a small plate and left in the freezer for 4 minutes. Pour into hot, sterilised jars, distributing the kernels evenly, and allow to cool before sealing tightly. The apricot kernels aren't meant to be eaten, but they give a lovely subtle, nutty flavour to the jam.

*'It's a good feeling to have those beautiful jars on the shelf, preserving what can be quite delicate and seasonal.'*

# VINI

## 'Italians drink local first, regional second and Italian third.'

Italian restaurants are equally patriotic and chauvinist. They don't automatically choose the cheapest and most commercial wines available, but often have them made for them by a local vineyard. The vino di casa is almost always a vino di zona: 'made in the area'.

We've adopted the same philosophy, working with the renowned Ross Hill Vineyard in the cool-climate Orange wine-growing district about 250 kilometres north-west of Sydney in NSW to create a number of Italian-inspired wines that complement our food. Ross Hill is situated on the gentle north-facing slopes of Griffin Rd, the vines planted in 1994. The wine industry in Orange is relatively new, but it's very exciting, and we're thrilled we can both support local wines on our list and also provide benchmark wines that showcase Italy's unique terroir.

Whenever anyone asks me where the house wine is from, I say 'Arancia', because arancia is Italian for 'orange', and it comes from Orange. Then they always ask me where Arancia is, because, let's face it, they've never heard of it. I say it's a tiny Italian region south of Sicily. Like, way south, in the southern hemisphere.

Here's a cheat sheet from Nina on key varietals and iconic wines to order when in Italy - or when travelling through our wine list.

### ABRUZZI E MOLISE
*White wine:* trebbiano
*Red wine:* montepulciano, barbera, sangiovese

### ARANCIA, NSW
*White wine:* chardonnay, pinot grigio, arneis
*Red wine:* rosato, shiraz, pinot nero, nebbiolo

### BASILICATA
*White wine:* greco, malvasia, moscato
*Red wine:* aglianico

### CALABRIA
*White wine:* greco bianco, mantonico
*Red wine:* gaglioppo

### CAMPANIA
*White wine:* fiano, Greco di Tufo, falanghina, falerno
*Red wine:* aglianico, piedirosso

### EMILIA-ROMAGNA
*White wine:* Albana di Romagna, trebbiano, malvasia
*Red wine:* lambrusco, sangiovese, barbarossa

### FRIULI-VENEZIA GIULIA
*White wine:* pinot grigio, pinot bianco, friulano
*Red wine:* ribolla nera, pignolo, refosco

### LAZIO
*White wine:* malvasia, trebbiano
*Red wine:* cesanese, sangiovese, montepulciano

### LIGURIA
*White wine:* vermentino, bosco, albarola, pigato
*Red wine:* dolcetto, rossese, sangiovese

### LOMBARDIA
*White wine:* pinot bianco, pinot grigio, chardonnay
*Red wine:* pinot nero, barbera, nebbiolo

**MARCHE**
*White wine:* verdicchio, trebbiano, malvasia
*Red wine:* sangiovese, montepulciano

**PIEMONTE**
*White wine:* moscato, arneis, cortese, erbaluce
*Red wine:* barbera, dolcetto, nebbiolo, freisa

**PUGLIA**
*White wine:* verdeca, bombino
*Red wine:* negroamaro, primitivo, malvasia nera

**SARDEGNA**
*White wine:* vermentino, torbato, nuragus, moscato
*Red wine:* cannonau, carignano, monica

**SICILIA**
*White wine:* inzolia, catarratto
*Red wine:* nero d'Avola, frappato

**TOSCANA**
*White wine:* trebbiano, malvasia, vernaccia
*Red wine:* Chianti, sangiovese

**TRENTINO-ALTO ADIGE**
*White wine:* garganega, trebbiano, Soave, prosecco
*Red wine:* merlot, cabernet, corvina, rondinella

**UMBRIA**
*White wine:* trebbiano, grechetto, verdelho
*Red wine:* sangiovese, ciliegiolo, sagrantino, canaiolo

**VAL D'AOSTA**
*White wine:* pinot gris
*Red wine:* dolcetto, nebbiolo

**VENETO**
*White wine:* garganega, trebbiano, Soave, prosecco
*Red wine:* Amarone della Valpolicella, Bardolino, corvina

------

*'Whenever anyone asks me where the house wine is from, I say 'Arancia', because arancia is Italian for 'orange', and it comes from Orange in NSW.'*

------

# FAVORITI

*Everyone has their favourites. These are my all-time favourite Café Sopra dishes, with wine matches and notes by Nina.*

**Piatto:** Affettati misti (page 41)

**Vino:** Pinot grigio. 'This crisp, refreshing white from Italy's north is perfect for cutting through the richness and fattiness of the sliced meats. My favourite is produced for us by Ross Hill Vineyard in the Central West of NSW.'

**Piatto:** Ox-heart tomatoes with mozzarella di bufala and basil (page 46)

**Vino:** Vermentino. 'It's summer; it's hot. There's nothing more refreshing than a Sardinian vermentino like the Cantina Gallura Piras - rich and golden with an intense, sun-ripened fruit flavour.'

**Piatto:** Pasta ragu al Bolognese (page 89)

**Vino:** Valpolicella. 'This is a no-brainer. You want something light, aromatic and ruby-red, with hints of cherry and berry and a light touch of acidity. The Viviani valpol from the Veneto is the perfect match.'

**Piatto:** Lamb ragu with penne, chilli and rosemary (page 107)

**Vino:** Chianti. 'We love our 100 per cent sangiovese chianti at Café Sopra; it tastes so Tuscan, so romantic, all warm and soft and earthy but still delicate, like the La Selvanella on our list.'

**Piatto:** Meatballs with bucatini and rich tomato sauce (page 96)

**Vino:** Barbera. 'I love this wine; I think of it as strong and earthy. 100 per cent barbera from Piemonte with intensely ripe fruit, medium tannins and pleasant acidity is a great match with pasta and meatballs.'

**Piatto:** Parmesan-crumbed chicken (page 146)

**Vino:** Soave. 'The grape is garganega, the region Verona, and the wine a delicious blend of citrus and nuts with an amazing richness and bold finish; it meets the chicken exactly halfway.'

**Piatto:** Roast pork belly with rosemary polenta (page 131)

**Vino:** Brunello di Montalcino. 'They call it the god of Tuscany, and you can see why. It's a wine that cannot even be released until five years after the harvest, so it's dense, earthy, with loads of rich fruit and a sort of wisdom and elegance behind the strength.'

**Piatto:** Tiramisu (page 231)

**Vino:** Passito. 'You don't think of Italy as the home of dessert wines, and yet passito, produced in the Veneto from garganega grapes, is deliciously sweet, with notes of candied apricot and citrus. The smell is like standing in an Italian pasticceria.'

**Piatto:** Zucchini flowers with five Italian cheeses (page 38)

**Vino:** Tenuta Ca' Vescovo prosecco. 'This is actually my favourite dish, not Barry's, but I've muscled it in here because it's so, so good. Have it with a beautiful prosecco made in the Veneto from glera grapes. It has a generous bead of bubbles, a pale straw colour and a crisp finish that nicely cuts through the richness of the cheeses. It's also beautiful matched to Pommery Brut, our classic, elegant house Champagne.'

**Piatto:** Pizza alla marinara (page 180)

**Vino:** Fratelli Fresh Pinot Nero. 'Our pinot nero is produced in Orange, NSW - or Arancia, as we call it. It's intensely aromatic, with beautiful soft flavours that work well with the oregano and anchovy without clashing or overpowering them.'

...ALSA DI POMOD...

RAISED LENTILS

# BASICS

GNOCCHI Green...

...ft Polenta...

...Lemon Vinaigr...

# AIOLI

**MAKES 400 G (14 OZ)**

*We make a pretty refined, mildly garlicky aioli, with influences from American mayonnaise and British salad cream. It's a ripper.*

**2 egg yolks**
**1 tbsp hot English mustard**
**3 tbsp white wine vinegar**
**400 ml (14 fl oz) vegetable oil**
**2 garlic cloves, finely sliced**
**1/2 onion, finely sliced**

To make the aioli, whiz the egg yolks, mustard and vinegar in a food processor until combined. With the motor running, gradually add the oil, drop by drop at first, then in a steady stream, until the mixture is thick and emulsified.

You can stop here, adding a splash of warm water if the mixture feels too thick, and store it in an airtight jar in the fridge - or continue for the special secret Café Sopra business.

Add 2½ tablespoons of warm water to the aioli, and fold in the garlic and onion. Cover and store in the fridge for 2 days to infuse, then strain out the garlic and onions through a sieve, season the aioli and store in an airtight jar in the fridge.

# BASIL OIL

**MAKES 300 ML (10½ FL OZ)**

*You can easily make your own herb oils at home - basil and parsley are particularly good - to drizzle over tomato salads, buffalo mozzarella, roast chicken, and delicate vegetable soups such as the fennel soup with scallops (page 62).*

**180 g (6 oz/3 cups, firmly packed) basil leaves**
**150 ml (5 fl oz) extra virgin olive oil**
**100 ml (3½ fl oz) grapeseed oil**

Bring a large saucepan of water to the boil. Blanch the basil for 20 seconds then quickly remove and plunge immediately into a bowl of ice-cold water. Drain well, squeeze dry and roughly chop. Whiz the basil in a blender with the olive oil and grapeseed oil, sea salt and freshly ground black pepper to a puree. You can use as is, or strain overnight through dampened muslin (cheesecloth) or a paper coffee filter set inside a funnel. Store in an airtight container in the fridge, and use within 7 days.

# BRAISED LENTILS

SERVES 4–6

*Lentils have an earthy goodness that makes them craving material. If you remember to soak them overnight, they take less than half an hour to cook until tender.*

**500 g (1 lb 2 oz) dried Puy or tiny blue-green lentils**
**1 onion, diced**
**1 carrot, diced**
**2 celery stalks, diced**
**1 tbsp thyme leaves**

Soak the lentils overnight in twice their volume of water, then drain.

Fill a large saucepan with 1.5 litres (52 fl oz/6 cups) of cold, unsalted water. Add the lentils, onion, carrot, celery and thyme. Bring to the boil, and simmer over low heat for 20-25 minutes or until the lentils and vegetables are tender. Add salt to the water for the last 5 minutes of cooking time, stirring well. Drain and cool the lentils and use as required.

# GARLIC CONFIT

MAKES 100 G (3½ OZ)

*Slow-cooking garlic cloves in oil takes out the harsh sting and gives them a mellow and nutty flavour.*

**100 g (3½ oz) garlic cloves**
**vegetable oil, to cover**

Place the garlic cloves in a small saucepan, cover with oil and place over very low heat. The garlic should not fry, but just barely move in the oil. When the cloves are very soft (about 45 minutes), remove the pan from the heat. Pick out the garlic and crush in a mortar and pestle. Transfer to an airtight jar, cover with the oil and store in the fridge.

# GNOCCHI

**SERVES 4**

*Gnocchi is all about potatoes, and potatoes change according to the weather conditions, but overall, I recommend the all-purpose desiree potato. It's a little waxy, not too wet, with a bit of residual sugar.*

**600 g (1 lb 5 oz) desiree potatoes, scrubbed, unpeeled**
**2 eggs**
**50 g (1³⁄₄ oz) parmesan, grated**
**200 g (7 oz) plain (all-purpose) flour**

Place the unpeeled potatoes in a saucepan, cover with water and simmer until tender.

Drain and peel the still-warm potatoes, then put them through a potato ricer, or mash with a potato masher in a bowl, but don't overwork. Beat in the eggs, 1 tablespoon of sea salt and the parmesan. Sift the flour over the top and fold through, forming a soft dough that comes away from the sides of the bowl (you may need a little more flour if your potato is wet).

Tip the gnocchi dough out onto a well-floured work bench, and divide into three. Roll out into 2 cm (³⁄₄ in) diameter sausages and cut at 2 cm (³⁄₄ in) intervals into little logs. Turn each piece cut-side up and use your finger to press lightly to create an indent (or place each piece on the tines of a fork and press gently down with your thumb, and roll off the fork). Repeat with the remaining dough.

Bring a large saucepan of salted water to a gentle simmer. Cook the gnocchi in batches until they return to the surface, leaving them a further 30 seconds after they float. Remove with a slotted spoon, drain on paper towel, and keep warm while cooking the remaining gnocchi. Serve according to your recipe.

# LEMON VINAIGRETTE

**MAKES 600 ML (21 FL OZ)**

*This makes a lot, because we use a lot. You can always halve the recipe, but trust me, if this is in the fridge, you'll love having it to hand for all sorts of things.*

**2 tbsp white wine**
**2 tbsp white wine vinegar**
**2 tbsp lemon juice**
**200 ml (7 fl oz) vegetable oil**
**200 ml (7 fl oz) extra virgin olive oil**

Use a hand whisk to combine all the ingredients, adding sea salt and freshly ground black pepper to taste. Store in the fridge for up to 4 days.

# GREMOLATA

**MAKES 3 TBSP**

*Garlic, parsley and lemon zest make up the classic gremolata, a traditional garnish for Milanese braised meats - but feel free to add it to pasta, meatballs and vinaigrettes as well.*

1 tbsp finely grated lemon zest
1 tsp crushed garlic
2 tbsp finely chopped flat-leaf parsley

Combine the zest, garlic and parsley, and scatter over the top of the finished dish just before serving.

# PESTO

**SERVES 6**

*Pesto is Liguria's heavenly scented gift to the world. Spoon into vegetable soups, over roasted vegetables, on warmed focaccia bread, and over pasta, gnocchi and risotto.*

120 g (4$^1/_4$ oz/2 cups, firmly packed) basil leaves
150 ml (5 fl oz) extra virgin olive oil
2 tbsp pine nuts
2 garlic cloves, crushed
100 g (3$^1/_2$ oz) parmesan or pecorino, grated

In a food processor or blender, process the basil, 125 ml (4 fl oz/½ cup) of the olive oil, the pine nuts, garlic and 1 teaspoon of sea salt to a paste. Transfer to a bowl and fold in the parmesan. Add the remaining olive oil, stirring, until you have the consistency you like. Store in an airtight jar in the fridge for up to 5 days. As you use it, top up the jar with extra virgin olive oil, to protect the pesto from the air, which will cause it to brown.

# SALSA DI POMODORO

**ENOUGH FOR 4 PIZZE**

*This is a good all-round, all-season way of making that all-important tomato salsa that is the first thing to go on your pizza dough. In summer, add a few chopped cherry tomatoes as well.*

**250 g (9 oz) tinned chopped tomatoes**
**2 tbsp chopped basil leaves**
**1 tsp dried oregano**
**1 tsp sea salt**
**2 tbsp extra virgin olive oil**
**1 tsp caster (superfine) sugar**

Combine all ingredients in a saucepan and simmer, stirring occasionally, for 10 minutes until the water content is reduced and the sauce is a bit thick and lumpy.

Blend in a food processor or blender until smooth. Store in the fridge until ready to use; it will keep for up to 3 days.

# SALSA VERDE

**MAKES 250 ML (9 FL OZ/1 CUP)**

*The quintessential Italian herb sauce, brilliant with boiled meats and grilled seafood.*

**50 g (1³/₄ oz) salted baby capers, rinsed**
**60 g (2¹/₄ oz) anchovies in oil, drained**
**2 garlic cloves, crushed**
**2 tsp dijon mustard**
**185 ml (6 fl oz/³/₄ cup) extra virgin olive oil, plus extra to cover**
**1 bunch flat-leaf parsley, leaves picked**

Process all ingredients except the parsley to a paste in a food processor. Add the parsley and process until you have a coarse paste. Store under a layer of extra virgin olive oil in a jar in the fridge for up to 3 days.

# SOFT POLENTA

**SERVES 4**

*Italy's answer to mashed potato - an oozy golden lava of hot cornmeal 'porridge' that soaks up slow-braised meat sauces and melting cheeses.*

**170 g (6 oz) instant polenta (cornmeal)**
**50 g (1¾ oz) unsalted butter**
**80 g (2¾ oz) parmesan, finely grated**

Bring 1 litre (35 fl oz/4 cups) of water and 2 teaspoons of salt to the boil in a saucepan. Whisking continuously, add the polenta in a slow stream and continue to whisk for 5 minutes or until it begins to thicken.

Reduce the heat to low and cook, beating with a wooden spoon to prevent it from catching on the base, for a further 5 minutes. Add the butter and parmesan, stir until melted then check for seasoning. Keep warm.

# SUGAR SYRUP

**MAKES 400 ML (14 FL OZ)**

*Having a batch of sugar syrup to hand is brilliant for cocktails and aperitivi, as you don't have to worry about the sugar not dissolving, and you can adjust the amount you add to suit your own taste. You can even turn it into a classic sour mix for use with certain aperitivi such as the Italian Sour on page 26, by mixing it with an equal quantity of lime or lemon juice.*

**200 g (7 oz) granulated sugar**

Combine the sugar and 300 ml (10½ fl oz) of water in a small saucepan and bring to the boil, stirring constantly. Simmer for 2 minutes, stirring occasionally, until the sugar is completely dissolved. Cool before using, and store in the fridge for up to 1 month.

# SWEET SHORTCRUST PASTRY

## MAKES 6 SMALL TARTS

*Making your own pastry is relatively easy, and makes the world of difference. This is perfect for the fig and almond tart on page 224.*

250 g (9 oz) plain (all-purpose) flour
100 g (3½ oz) icing (confectioners') sugar, sifted
50 g (1¾ oz) almond meal
100 g (3½ oz) unsalted butter, chilled
1 egg
1 egg yolk

Process the flour, sugar, almond meal and butter in a food processor until the mixture resembles breadcrumbs. Add the whole egg and egg yolk and process until the mixture just comes together. Form into a ball, wrap in plastic wrap and refrigerate for 1 hour.

Heat the oven to 180°C (350°F). Roll out the pastry on a lightly floured bench and use it to line 6 small loose-based flan (tart) tins. Refrigerate for 10 minutes then line the pastry with baking paper and fill with dried beans or pastry weights. Place on a baking tray and bake for 10 minutes, then remove the paper and beans and bake for a further 5 minutes or until the pastry is dry and pale golden. Cool in the tins before filling and baking according to the recipe.

# VEGETABLE STOCK

## MAKES 1.5 LITRES (52 FL OZ)

*This makes a light, fresh base for soups, sauces and risotto. By all means add whatever vegetables you have around - broccoli, fennel or button mushrooms. Make ahead and freeze in small batches so you can call on it whenever you need it.*

2 onions, roughly chopped
2 carrots, roughly chopped
2 stalks celery, roughly chopped
2 tomatoes, roughly chopped
6 parsley stalks, roughly chopped
2 bay leaves
1 tsp whole black peppercorns

Combine the vegetables, herbs and peppercorns in a large saucepan and add 1.5 litres (52 fl oz/6 cups) of cold water, or enough to just cover. Bring to just under the boil, stirring, then cover, reduce the heat to low and simmer gently for 45 minutes. Strain the stock through a sieve, cool and refrigerate or freeze. For a more intense stock, boil the strained liquid until reduced by half, then cool and refrigerate or freeze.

# GRAZIE

Fratelli Fresh is first and foremost a family business, so my biggest thanks of all go out to my family - to my wife Karen and daughters Nina and Grace, who are always there when I need them, which is pretty much all the time. Nina has grown into the business from day one; our skills complement each other and, to me, she is the future of Fratelli Fresh, especially now that she and Justin have brought little Jesse into the world - although I would like to note that he's now several months old and still hasn't done his first dinner service at Café Sopra.

To my brother Jamie, who helped me set up the business in the first place, and to my father Tom, who still makes his amazing jams for us to this day, thanks for everything. I would also like to thank Nick Peters, Simon Mordant and Les Schirato for their support and guidance over the years.

Then there is my other family, all the skilled and dedicated people who cook the food, stock the shelves, serve the customers, manage the front of house and generally keep the wheels turning at Sydney's five Fratelli Fresh and Café Sopra locations, as well as at Café Nice in Circular Quay. We rarely have a slow day in this business, and their non-stop energy and commitment to keeping our customers happy is key to our success.

There's another family, too, that nobody gets to see - a dedicated team of growers, farmers and producers that stretches across NSW and Australia, making sure we have the very best of fresh, seasonal produce. I've been working with some of them from the day I started business. We also have brilliant Italian suppliers of everything from cheese to olive oil, vinegar and mozzarella; their belief in what they do means a lot to me.

Special mention goes to our talented head chef, Sean Corkery, and his team, who not only compiled all these recipes but tested them in a domestic kitchen (mine) to make sure they would work for everyone at home, and then made them all over again for the photography for the book.

Thanks, too, to my newest family, the team at Murdoch Books, from group publishing director Sue Hines to publisher Corinne Roberts, editorial manager Virginia Birch, editor Melissa Penn, design manager Viv Valk and designer Vivien Sung. Together with our gifted photographer Rob Palmer and stylish stylist Vanessa Austin, they really captured the 'Sydney/Italian' way we do things at Fratelli Fresh.

And a final thank-you to Terry Durack and Jill Dupleix for suggesting we do the book in the first place. We simply wouldn't have done the book if you guys were not involved, and we value your creative and professional input. Thanks, Terry, for turning our series of interviews over the odd glass of wine into something good to read.

One more thank you, then I'm off for a Campari. The most important people to me are those who come to Fratelli Fresh every day of the year, to sit down to a crusty pizza and a glass of wine, or to pick up some fruit and a cheese to take home. I hope you all enjoy this book - but not so much that you stay home and cook instead of coming to Fratelli Fresh.

*Barry*

# INDEX

Published in 2015 by Murdoch Books,
an imprint of Allen & Unwin

Murdoch Books Australia
83 Alexander Street
Crows Nest NSW 2065
Phone: +61 (0) 2 8425 0100
Fax: +61 (0) 2 9906 2218
murdochbooks.com.au
info@murdochbooks.com.au

Murdoch Books UK
Erico House, 6th Floor
93-99 Upper Richmond Road
Putney, London SW15 2TG
Phone: +44 (0) 20 8785 5995
murdochbooks.co.uk
info@murdochbooks.co.uk

For Corporate Orders & Custom Publishing contact
Noel Hammond, National Business Development Manager,
Murdoch Books Australia

Publishing Consultants: Jill Dupleix and Terry Durack
Publisher: Corinne Roberts
Editorial Manager: Virginia Birch
Design Manager: Vivien Valk
Editor: Melissa Penn
Designer: Vivien Sung
Photographer: Rob Palmer
Stylist: Vanessa Austin
Stylist's Assistant: Naomi van Groll
Production Manager: Mary Bjelobrk

ISBN 978 1 74336 470 3 Australia
ISBN 978 1 74336 471 0 UK

A catalogue record for this book is available from the British
Library.

Colour reproduction by Splitting Image Colour Studio Pty Ltd,
Clayton, Victoria
Printed by C & C Offset Printing Co. Ltd., China

IMPORTANT: Those who might be at risk from the effects of
salmonella poisoning (the elderly, pregnant women, young
children and those suffering from immune deficiency diseases)
should consult their doctor with any concerns about eating
raw eggs.

OVEN GUIDE: You may find cooking times vary depending on
the oven you are using. For fan-forced ovens, as a general rule,
set the oven temperature to 20°C (35°F) lower than indicated in
the recipe.

MEASURES GUIDE: We have used 20 ml (4 teaspoon) tablespoon
measures. If you are using a 15 ml (3 teaspoon) tablespoon add an
extra teaspoon of the ingredient for each tablespoon specified.